MONS 1914

MONS 1914

DAVID LOMAS

ED DOVEY

OSPREY
HISTORY

First published in Great Britain in 1997 by Osprey Publishing,
Elms Court, Chapel Way, Botley, Oxford OX2 9LP
United Kingdom
Email: info@ospreypublishing.com

Also published as Campaign 49 *Mons 1914*

ISBN 1 84176 142 7

Military Editor: Sharon van der Merwe
Design: The Black Spot

Colour bird's eye view illustrations by Peter Harper
Cartography by Micromap
Wargaming Mons by Ian Drury
Battlescene artwork by Ed Dovey
Filmset in Singapore by Pica Ltd.
Printed in China through World Print Ltd.

FRONT COVER: Retreat from Mons, the British Cavalry Retiring.
(Imperical War Museum, photo number Q60695)

BACK COVER: The German Model 96 field gun with a crew from the 4th
Bavarian Royal Field Artillery Regiment. (Author's Collection)

FOR A CATALOGUE OF ALL BOOKS PUBLISHED BY OSPREY
MILITARY, AUTOMOTIVE AND AVIATION PLEASE WRITE TO:

The Marketing Manager, Osprey Direct UK, PO Box 140,
Wellingborough, Northants, NN8 4ZA, United Kingdom
Email: info@ospreydirect.co.uk

The Marketing Manager, Osprey Direct USA, PO Box 130, Sterling
Heights, MI 48311-0130, United States of America
Email: info@ospreydirectusa.com

Dedicated to John Terraine, like Thucydides, an historian

Acknowledgements

The list of people who helped this title to materialise is legion; but
special mention must be made of Jules Brihay and his staff of the
Department of Tourism and Culture at Mons, from whom many of
the photographs in this book were obtained, as well as the Imperial
War Museum, whose staff once more lived up to their legendary
reputation for outstanding helpfulness and courtesy. Finally, this
title would have been completed in half the time without the enthusiastic assistance of Beyaz Bardem, mother of beautiful kittens, and
an expert at sitting on keyboards.

Editorial Note

The editor would like to thank Mike Chappell and Martin Pegler for
their invaluable contribution to this book.

KEY TO MILITARY SYMBOLS

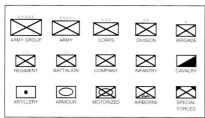

CONTENTS

ORIGINS OF THE CAMPAIGN

'We're off to fight the bloody Belgians!' an enthusiastic British soldier informed an astonished listener in the first, exciting days of August 1914. The European war, so long predicted, so long feared, had come at last, sparked by a handful of shots fired by a consumptive Serbian nationalist in Sarajevo.

The *Entente Cordiale* between Britain and France was little more than an understanding of mutual support should war come. The British had, though, given an assurance that the Royal Navy would not allow a foreign fleet into the English Channel and there was a further unspoken assumption that a British Expeditionary Force would help repel an invader from French soil.

Henry Wilson, who became Director of Military Operations in 1910, was an obsessive Francophile. Entirely on his own initiative, he promised the French that a British Expeditionary Force of six infantry divisions and one cavalry division would be sent to France. Under Wilson's guidance, mobilisation plans were produced with a single aim – to get the BEF across the Channel quickly enough to join a French offensive planned to start 15 days after mobilisation. The French courteously dubbed Wilson's scheme 'Plan W'.

On the afternoon of 5 August 1914, Herbert Asquith, the British Prime Minister, presided over a hastily arranged Council of War and discovered that Plan W was the only one available and capable of implementation. One change was made: two divisions – the 4th and the 6th – were kept back against the threat of a German invasion of Britain.

A British Expeditionary Force of four infantry divisions and one cavalry division supported by an extra cavalry brigade would go to war. It would be commanded by Sir John French; the four infantry divisions would form

LEFT **British troops, probably of the 8th Brigade, II Corps, resting on their way to Mons. Note the cobbled paved road surface which caused a good deal of discomfort to many soldiers. (Mons Museum)**

BELOW **12 August 1914 – The 1st Battalion Grenadier Guards march out from Chelsea Barracks. (Private Collection)**

German Guard Infantry in Berlin entraining for the front, August 1914. (Private Collection)

The German Model 96 field gun, seen here with a crew from the 4th Bavarian Royal Field Artillery Regiment, created severe problems for the BEF in the first months of the war. It was an ominous portent for what proved to be a war in which artillery caused the greatest casualties. (Author's Collection)

I Corps, commanded by Sir Douglas Haig, and II Corps would be under Sir James Grierson. Major-General Allenby had command of the Cavalry Division.

A few days later, Sir John French received his instructions from Lord Kitchener, the War Minister, and one of the few men who anticipated a long struggle. Kitchener had little faith in Sir John French's abilities and distrusted Henry Wilson. His words reflected this concern. Sir John French was 'to support and co-operate with the French Army... in preventing or repelling the invasion by Germany of French and Belgian territory and eventually to restore the neutrality of Belgium'. The instructions continued: 'It must be recognised from the outset that the numerical strength of the British Force... is strictly limited... the greatest care must be exercised towards a minimum of losses and wastage. Therefore, while every effort must be made to coincide most sympathetically with the plans and wishes of our Ally, the gravest consideration will devolve upon you as to participation in forward movements where large bodies of French troops are not engaged and where your Force may be unduly exposed to attack. In this connection I wish you distinctly to understand that your command is an entirely independent one, and that you will in no case come in any sense under the orders of any Allied General.'

They were phrases to make anyone pause. The BEF was to help throw back one million Germans and restore Belgian independence, but to avoid heavy losses while doing so. It was to be part of French plans, yet remain independent despite the fact that it was only one-thirtieth the size of the French army, and was operating on French soil and relying on French goodwill for railways and rolling stock, accommodation, communication and supply lines, and myriad other requirements. It was hardly a promising start.

Feldkanone 96 n/A (Uniformierung feldgrau)

THE OPPOSING COMMANDERS

Field Marshal Sir John French had resigned from his position as Chief of the Imperial General Staff in 1914 in protest over the Government's Irish Home Rule Bill. When war was declared, he was offered command of the BEF. Quick-tempered to the point of explosive, French was personally brave and much liked by his men. (Author's Collection)

RIGHT II Corps was originally under the command of Sir John Grierson; Grierson died suddenly on 17 August 1914 and Kitchener chose Sir Horace Smith-Dorrien to replace him. This was a move directly contrary to the expressed wish of Sir John French. Kitchener distrusted French and Smith-Dorrien loathed each other. Smith-Dorrien was, nonetheless, a very considerable soldier and his admirers will always remain convinced that it was his actions which saved the BEF from certain disaster during August 1914.

THE BRITISH COMMANDERS

Field Marshal Sir John French was 62 years old in August 1914 and had an outstanding record of distinguished service, being one of the few senior officers who enhanced his reputation during the South African War.

French was a cavalryman, and not at heart a staff officer but a fighting soldier, a quality which endeared him to his troops and gained both their respect and affection. He went to France full of confidence, convinced that he could lead the BEF to a part in a swift and decisive victory. French had a hot temper and was quick to take offence; he harboured grudges. Worse, for a commander, he suffered from mercurial changes of mood, plunging from enormous optimism to deep pessimism in a matter of moments.

General Sir Douglas Haig, commanding I Corps, was another highly regarded officer. As a pre-war Director of Military Training, Haig was not only the architect of Field Service Regulations which essentially prepared the British Army for a European war, but he had also been responsible for the organisation and training of the Territorial Army. Naturally shy, Haig was not a fluent speaker and was often tongue-tied in debate, a drawback which was to cause him many problems. He was, nonetheless, a very capable soldier who believed firmly in total attention to detail, and close and constant co-operation between all arms. Haig had the respect

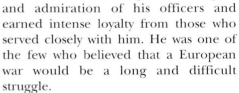

and admiration of his officers and earned intense loyalty from those who served closely with him. He was one of the few who believed that a European war would be a long and difficult struggle.

General Sir Horace Smith-Dorrien was sent to command II Corps by Kitchener when Grierson died shortly after the war began. His appointment was against the wishes of Sir John French, as the two officers disliked each other intensely. Smith-Dorrien was more of a regimental soldier than many of his contemporaries, serving for much of his career with the Sherwood Foresters, an unfashionable but hard-fighting infantry regiment. He fought in the Zulu War in 1879 (during which he was recommended for, but did not receive, the

Victoria Cross), in the Tirah and Sudan campaigns, and in South Africa. Prone to uncontrollable outbursts of rage, he was a pugnacious soldier with an independent turn of mind.

THE FRENCH COMMANDERS

General Charles Lanrezac was 62 when he took command of the French Fifth Army. He was the man who would work most closely with the BEF. He was remarkably intelligent and brilliantly logical in his assessments; qualities which counterbalanced his tendency to bad temper, sarcastic comment and swearing. He became a controversial figure. To many French commentators, his decision to to retreat from the advancing Germans in August 1914 was extremely shrewd and saved the only intact army France possessed. Without it the Marne could not have been won. To the British, his withdrawal without warning them was a betrayal of an ally and a betrayal which placed the BEF in acute danger.

THE GERMAN COMMANDERS

Alexander von Kluck, commander of the German First Army, had an overweening belief in his own abilities, and thought, not unjustifiably, his role to be the most important in the execution of the Schlieffen Plan. The First Army was the one which had to march the farthest and needed a ruthless commander dedicated to success. Von Kluck was extremely conscious of the rewards that a successful outcome would bring him per-sonally. Obsessed with his own glory, his judgement was flawed. With a penchant for ignoring orders with which he did not agree, and an abrasive personality, von Kluck was a difficult man to deal with. The German cause was not helped by his detestation of the commander of the neighbouring Second Army.

Karl von Bulow commanded the Second Army. He was not a resolute character, and the worries of high command made him depressed and anxious. He had earned a reputation in pre-war manoeuvres for his cautious tactics and the great importance he attached to units giving each other elaborate mutual support. Unable to get co-operation from von Kluck, he resorted to seeking the support of Supreme Headquarters on any point of difference between them, a procedure which came close to wrecking the advance.

General von Bulow, commander of the German Second Army, detested von Kluck and the feeling was certainly mutual. For a campaign in which close co-operation between the two armies was essential, this personal dislike was to have disastrous consequences. Von Bulow's caution and von Kluck's determination caused great problems once the war had begun. Von Bulow considered the defeat of the BEF to be entirely a matter for von Kluck and he therefore ignored any reports of the British movements as being irrelevant to his own. Von Kluck, in turn, either ignored or disobeyed orders or requests which came from von Bulow. (Author's Collection)

THE OPPOSING ARMIES

THE BRITISH

The tiny volunteer British Army of 1914 was not generally representative of the country as a whole. In many regiments officers needed a private income as it was almost impossible to live on the pay alone. An officer provided his own uniforms, cases, furniture and servant's outfit; there were mess contributions, field sports and social events. In the Cameronians, a private income of about £250 per year would suffice; the Guards anticipated that £400 a year was required. Cavalry regiments were even more expensive – a charger was essential, as were two hunters and three polo ponies.

Nearly half of all recruits to the ranks were registered as unskilled labourers on enlistment. Even those claiming a trade when joining were often unemployed. Many came from the slums of the industrial towns, were usually under-nourished and only just met the medical standard – 5ft 3in tall, 33in chest and 112 pounds in weight.

Barrack accommodation ranged from adequate to abysmal. Soldiers had no privacy and often ate in the rooms in which they slept. This was still an improvement on the slums of their home town, for their surroundings were clean, they received regular, if low, wages, adequate meals and were also educated, if necessary, at the Army's expense.

A spirit of common endeavour had developed from the reforms of the late Victorian age. Officers were encouraged to work closely with the

French carabiniers in 1914. In their near-Napoleonic uniforms, these cavalrymen were photographed shortly after mobilisation waiting at the Paris Gare du Nord railway station. Armed with the sabre and a carbine which was described as 'no more than a pop-gun', the French cavalry had the habit of riding everywhere at the expense of their horses. A British cavalry officer noted with distaste that he could smell a group of French cavalry from a distance of 400 metres because of the saddle sores and the ungroomed state of their mounts. The British cavalry trooper was accustomed to walk as much as he rode and to keep his horse groomed, fed and cared for before himself if need be. (Private Collection)

RIGHT & BELOW RIGHT **British infantrymen on the pre-1914 precursor of the modern assault course. Under the influence of Haldane, Haig and others, British Army training in the early years of the 20th century sought to instill not just physical fitness but a sense of self-reliance into the private soldier. (Author's Collection)**

non-commissioned officers and to know their men. NCOs took much responsibility for the daily routine and training, and provided a vital link between the officer and the private soldier. Officers and men had a common bond in loyalty to their regiment.

Training was carefully planned, moving throughout the year from individual and platoon skills during the winter, to company and battalion exercises in the spring, brigade and divisional manoeuvres in the summer and a full army exercise in the autumn. There was particular emphasis on marksmanship and marching.

Shortage of money concentrated training on what was believed to be the immediate reality for the Army – the small colonial conflict, or a short war of movement in Europe. There was little expectation that there would be prolonged trench or siege warfare, and the British Army was neither equipped nor trained to deal with that eventuality.

In May 1914, the Regular Army was about 11,000 men short of its peacetime establishment of 260,000 men. The number of full-time soldiers in Britain, including recruits under training, was 137,000. The remainder were in the overseas garrisons of the British Empire. There were not nearly enough men to supply the number needed for the 48 infantry battalions, 16 cavalry regiments, five batteries of horse artillery, 16 brigades of field artillery, four heavy artillery batteries, eight field companies of engineers and motley collection of support services which the Expeditionary Force required.

German horse artilleryman, 1914. This studio portrait shows a Saxon soldier of von Hausen's Third Army which only marginally came into contact with the BEF in the very first days of the war. Later, at Ypres and elsewhere, it was to be a very different story. (Author's Collection)

The answer to the conundrum was the Reservist. Most men left the army after seven years and then served on the Reserve for a further five. Recalled by letter, telegram and public notices, some 70,000 men poured into regimental depots to bring a woefully under-strength British Army on to a war footing. In some units, more than 60 per cent of the men who were to sail to France were Reservists. One infantry battalion embodied 734 Reservists to bring it up to its war establishment of 992 men. Every unit had its complement of men who had served in South Africa, China, India, Burma and a score of other Imperial stations. Old soldiers they may have been, but their time away from the Army had inevitably softened them. There would later be a price to pay under a blazing sun on the dusty roads of France and Belgium.

THE FRENCH

When mobilised, the French Army had more than one million men, and over three million if the Territorials and surplus Reservists were included. A French conscript served for three years, but his reserve training was virtually non-existent.

The French Army, too, suffered from parsimonious politicians. The infantry were still uniformed very much as they had been in the Franco-Prussian War, with blue tunics and bright red trousers. The cavalry looked almost exactly as their predecessors had done at Waterloo, particularly the cuirassiers with horsehair plumes trailing from crested helmets, steel breastplates and high boots. The uniforms appealed to the advocates of the offensive strategy. They felt it displayed the élan which was the special attribute of the French soldier. The economy involved in not providing the French soldier with a drab-coloured field service uniform became a positive virtue.

Training also recalled the days of Napoleon. The infantry were expected to advance in a solid mass, the cavalry to charge with lance and sabre, tactics which demanded a rigid and unthinking discipline. The ordinary soldier was required to do no more than to obey orders promptly and to advance with spirit when commanded. Their officers, as one observer recorded, 'were entirely ignorant of the stopping power of modern firearms and many of them thought it chic to die in white gloves'.

The French field artillery was superb. It was to prove itself time and time again, its quick-firing 75mm gun being one of the finest in service throughout the war. The field artillery was the one redeeming feature of an army equipped and trained, in many respects, for the campaigns of the first Napoleon.

THE GERMANS

The German Army was a carefully structured organisation, designed to muster, with reserves, more than 5 million men when fully mobilised. At its heart was a well-trained officer corps, supported by 100,000 highly professional non-commissioned officers, who imposed a rigid discipline and demanded unquestioning obedience from its rank and file.

At the age of 17, every German male became liable for service in the *Landsturm*, the organisation for home defence. At 20, the man moved to the active Army, serving two years in the infantry or three years in the cavalry and horse artillery. At the end of this time, he went to the reserve for four or five years, followed by 11 years in the *Landwehr* and eventually back to the *Landsturm* at the age of 39. Throughout his reserve service, there were two annual training periods.

The number of men available annually far exceeded Army requirements. More than one million reported for service each year of which only one-third were needed. This enabled the Army to pick the very best available men for active duty while turning over many thousands to the supplementary or Ersatz Reserve. The Ersatz Reserve yielded over one million reinforcements during the first three months of the war.

In its training, the German Army, unlike its British and French contemporaries, prepared for a European war. Observers were struck by an insistence on speed and the fierce march discipline – an essential requirement if the Schlieffen Plan was to adhere to its schedule. The infantry were trained in enveloping tactics, and to attack in dense waves at 500-metre intervals, supported by artillery and machine gun fire: such German assaults appeared unstoppable. Attacks were made in crescent formation, the enemy's flanks being overlapped and encircled while the centre was kept busy.

German commanders believed in the interdependence of all arms, a theory they emphasised by including Jaeger battalions and horse artillery in the cavalry divisions. Under pressure, German cavalry were able to pull back to the protection provided by their own machine guns and field pieces.

Size alone made the German Army a very formidable opponent. Trained to a high level, with an exceptionally professional officer corps, its rigid hierarchy discouraged delegation and inhibited individual initiative not only in the lower echelons, but among regimental and brigade commanders and even divisional and corps commanders. It was a failing that would only become significant if the plans, rehearsed to perfection on so many annual peacetime manoeuvres, went awry – and the German General Staff did not intend that they should.

ORDERS OF BATTLE

The Orders of Battle do not, for reasons of clarity, include support and lines of communications troops, e.g. Royal Army Medical Corps, Army Service Corps, GHQ troops etc. The French and Belgian Orders of Battle have not been included.

THE BRITISH EXPEDITIONARY FORCE
AUGUST 1914

Commander-in-Chief: Field-Marshal Sir J.D.P French, GCB, GCVO, KCMG
Chief of the General Staff: Lieutenant-General Sir A.J. Murray, KCB, CVO, DSO
Major-General, General Staff: Major-General H.H. Wilson, CB, DSO
GSOi (Intelligence): Colonel G.M.W. Macdonogh
Quartermaster-General: Major-General Sir W.R. Robertson, KCVO, CB, DSO

THE CAVALRY DIVISION
Major-General E.H. Allenby, CB

IST CAVALRY BRIGADE
Brigadier-General C.J. Briggs, CB
2nd Dragoon Guards (Queen's Bays)
5th (Princess Charlotte of Wales') Dragoon Guards
11th (Prince Albert's Own) Hussars

2ND CAVALRY BRIGADE
Brigadier-General H. de B. de Lisle, CB, DSO
4th (Royal Irish) Dragoon Guards
9th (Queen's Royal) Lancers
18th (Queen Mary's Own) Hussars

3RD CAVALRY BRIGADE
Brigadier-General H. de la P. Gough, CB
4th (Queen's Own) Hussars
5th (Royal Irish) Lancers
16th (The Queen's) Lancers

4TH CAVALRY BRIGADE
Brigadier-General Hon. C.E. Bingham, CVO. CB
Composite Regiment of Household Cavalry
6th Dragoon Guards (Carabiniers)
3rd (King's Own) Hussars

5TH CAVALRY BRIGADE
GOC: Brigadier-General Sir P.W. Chetwode, Bart,. DSO
2nd Dragoons (Royal Scots Greys)
12th Lancers
20th Hussars
'D', 'E', 'I', 'J', 'L' Batteries, RHA

I CORPS
GOC: Lieutenant-General Sir D. Haig, KCB, KCIE, KCVO, ADC-Gen.
BGGS: Brigadier-General J.E. Gough, VC, CMG, ADC

IST DIVISION
Major-General S.H. Lomax

1st (Guards) Brigade
Brigadier-General F.I. Maxse, CVO, CB, DSO
1/Coldstream Guards
1/Scots Guards
1/Black Watch
2/Royal Munster Fusiliers

2ND DIVISION
Major-General C.C. Monro, CB

4th (Guards) Brigade
Brigadier-General R. Scott-Kerr, CB, MVO, DSO
2/Grenadier Guards
2/Coldstream Guards
3/Coldstream Guards
1/Irish Guards

The popular image of the German soldier. A private of the 40th Infantry in 1914. (Author's Collection)

The bicycling craze which began in the last years of Queen Victoria's reign had its effect on military thinking. German, Belgian, French and British armies all had specialist cycle troops who could use their mounts to move silently upon an enemy. Special bicycle tactics were introduced and the cycle-equipped soldier was looked upon as a pseudo-cavalryman – he could ride ahead and act as a scout. The lance-corporal appears to have lost his cap badge but his service issue mug is firmly attached to the front handlebars. (Private Collection)

I CORPS continued

2nd Brigade
Brigadier-General E.S. Bulfin, CVO, CB
2/Royal Sussex Regiment
1/Loyal North Lancashire Regiment
1/Northamptonshire Regiment
2/King's Royal Rifle Corps

5th Brigade
Brigadier-General R.C.B. Haking, CB
2/Oxfordshire & Buckinghamshire Light Infantry
2/Worcester Regiment
2/Highland Light Infantry
2/Connaught Rangers

3rd Brigade
Brigadier-General H.J.S. Landon, CB
1/Queen's (Royal West Surrey Regiment)
1/South Wales Borderers
1/Gloucester Regiment
2/Welch Regiment
'A' Squadron, 15th Hussars
XXV (113th, 114th, 115th Batteries),
XXVI (116th, 117th, 118th Batteries),
XXXIX (46th, 51st, 54th Batteries),
XLIII (30th, 40th, 57th (How) Batteries)
Brigades RFA
26th Heavy Battery, RGA
23rd, 26th Field Companies, RE

6th Brigade
Brigadier-General R.H. Davies, CB (NZ Staff Corps)
1/King's (Liverpool Regiment)
2/South Staffordshire Regiment
1/Royal Berkshire Regiment
1/King's Royal Rifle Corps
'B' Squadron, 15th Hussars
XXXIV (22nd, 50th, 70th Batteries),
XXXVI (15th, 48th, 71st Batteries),
XLI (9th, 16th, 17th Batteries),
XLIV (47th, 56th, 60th (Howitzer) Batteries)
Brigades RFA
35th Heavy Battery, RGA
5th, 11th Field Companies RE

II CORPS
GOC: Lieutenant-General Sir J.M. Grierson, KCB, CVO, CMG, ADC-Gen. (Died 17 August 1914)
General Sir H.L. Smith-Dorrien, GCB, DSO (assumed command 21 August)
BGGS: Brigadier-General G.T. Forestier-Walker, ADC

3RD DIVISION
Major-General H.I.W. Hamilton, CVO, CB, DSO

5TH DIVISION
Maj.-General Sir C. Fergusson, Bart., CB, MVO, DSO

7th Brigade
Brigadier-General F.W.N. McCracken, CB, DSO
3/Worcester Regiment
2/South Lancashire Regiment
1/Wiltshire Regiment
2/Royal Irish Rifles

13th Brigade
Brigadier-General G.J. Cuthbert, CB
2/King's Own Scottish Borderers
2/Duke of Wellington's (West Riding Regiment)
1/Queen's Own (Royal West Kent Regiment)
2/King's Own (Yorkshire Light Infantry)

8th Brigade
Brigadier-General B.J.C. Doran
2/Royal Scots
2/Royal Irish Regiment
4/Middlesex Regiment
1/Gordon Highlanders

14th Brigade
Brigadier-General S.P. Rolt, CB
2/Suffolk Regiment
1/East Surrey Regiment
1/Duke of Cornwall's Light Infantry
2/Manchester Regiment

9th Brigade
Brigadier-General F.C. Shaw, CB
1/Northumberland Fusiliers
4/Royal Fusiliers
1/Lincolnshire Regiment
1/Royal Scots Fusiliers
'C' Squadron, 15th Hussars
XXIII (107th, 108th, 109th Batteries),
XL (6th, 23rd, 49th Batteries),
XLII (29th, 41st, 45th Batteries),
XXX (Howitzer) (128th, 129th, 130th (Howitzer)
Batteries) Brigades, RFA
48th Heavy Battery, RGA
56th, 57th Field Companies, RE

15th Brigade
Brigadier-General
A.E.W. Count Gleichen, KCVO, CB, CMG, DSO
1/Norfolk Regiment
1/Bedfordshire Regiment
1/Cheshire Regiment
Dorsetshire Regiment
'A' Squadron, 19th Hussars
XV (11th, 52nd, 80th Batteries),
XXVII (119th, 120th, 121st Batteries),
XXVIII (122nd, 123rd, 124th Batteries),
VIII (Howitzer) (37th, 61st, 65th (Howitzer)
Batteries) Brigades, RFA
108th Heavy Battery, RGA
17th, 59th Field Companies, RE

III CORPS

GOC: Major-General W.P. Pulteney, CB, DSO
BGGS: Brigadier-General J.P. Du Cane, CB

4TH DIVISION

GOC: Major-General T.D'O. Snow, CB

10th Brigade
Brigadier-General J.A.L. Haldane, CB, DSO
1/Royal Warwickshire Regiment
2/Seaforth Highlanders
1/Irish Fusiliers
2/Royal Dublin Fusiliers

11th Brigade
Brigadier-General A.G. Hunter-Weston, CB, DSO
1/Somerset Light Infantry
1/East Lancashire Regiment
1/Hampshire Regiment
1/Rifle Brigade

12th Brigade
Brigadier-General H.F.M. Wilson, CB
1/King's Own (Royal Lancaster Regiment)
2/Lancashire Fusiliers
2/Royal Inniskilling Fusiliers
2/Essex Regiment
'B' Squadron, 19th Hussars
XIV (39th, 68th, 88th Batteries),
XXIX (125th, 126th, 127th Batteries),
XXXII (27th, 134th, 135th Batteries),
XXXVII (Howitzer) (31st, 35th, 55th Howitzer
Batteries) Brigades, RFA
31st Heavy Battery, RGA
7th, 9th Field Companies, RE

19th Brigade
Major-General L.G. Drummond, CB, MVO
2/Royal Welch Fusiliers
1/Cameronians
1/Middlesex Regiment
2/Argyll & Sutherland Highlanders

ROYAL FLYING CORPS

Brigadier-General Sir D. Henderson, KCB, DSO

2nd Aeroplane Squadron
3rd Aeroplane Squadron
4th Aeroplane Squadron
5th Aeroplane Squadron
1st Aircraft Park

Annual training, 1910. The German system ensured that reserve troops received two weeks of annual training each year. This group were photographed in their old Prussian blue uniforms in the summer of 1910 shortly before receiving their new field-grey dress. (Author's Collection)

Commander of the German II Cavalry Corps, which consisted of the 2nd, 4th, and 9th Cavalry Divisions, von Marwitz was a competent commander whose men were sent off on a wild-goose chase towards the Channel coast to cut off what von Kluck believed would be the British line of retreat. At Néry on 1 September 1914, the 4th Cavalry Division became involved in one of the classic small-unit actions. (Private Collection)

ORDER OF BATTLE GERMAN ARMIES 1914

Chief of the General Staff: Generaloberst von Moltke
Deputy Chief of the General Staff: General von Stein

FIRST ARMY
General von Kluck

II CORPS
General von Lisengen

3RD DIVISION		4TH DIVISION	
5th Brigade	**6th Brigade**	**7th Brigade**	**8th Brigade**
2 Grenadier Rgt	34 Fusilier Rgt	14 Infantry Rgt	49 Infantry Rgt
9 Grenadier Rgt	42 Infantry Rgt	149 Infantry Rgt	140 Infantry Rgt

Cavalry 3 Horse Grenadier Rgt
Artillery 3 Bde: 2 F.A. Rgt
38 F.A. Rgt

Cavalry 12 Dragoon Rgt
Artillery 4 Bde: 17 F.A. Rgt
53 F.A. Rgt

III CORPS
General von Lochow

5TH DIVISION		6TH DIVISION	
9th Brigade	**10th Brigade**	**11th Brigade**	**12th Brigade**
8 Body Grenadier Rgt	12 Grenadier Rgt	20 Infantry Rgt	24 Infantry Rgt
48 Infantry Rgt	52 Infantry Rgt	35 Fusiliers Rgt	64 Infantry Rgt

Cavalry 3 Hussar Rgt (3 Sqns)
Artillery 18 F.A. Rgt, 54 F.A. Rgt

3 Jaeger Battalion
Cavalry 3 Hussars Rgt (3 Sqns)
Artillery 6 Bde: 3 F.A. Rgt, 39 F.A. Rgt

IV CORPS
General Sixt von Armin

7TH DIVISION		8TH DIVISION	
13th Brigade	**14th Brigade**	**15th Brigade**	**16th Brigade**
26 Infantry Rgt	27 Infantry Rgt	36 Fusiliers Rgt	72 Infantry Rgt
66 Infantry Rgt	165 Infantry Rgt	93 Infantry Rgt	153 Infantry Rgt

Cavalry 10 Hussars Rgt (3 Sqns)
Artillery 7 Bde: 4 F.A. Rgt, 40 F.A. Rgt

Cavalry 10 Hussars Rgt (3 Sqns)
Artillery 8 Bde: 74 F.A. Rgt, 75 F.A. Rgt

IX CORPS
General von Quast

17TH DIVISION		18TH DIVISION	
33 Brigade	**34 Brigade**	**35 Brigade**	**36 Brigade**
75 Infantry Rgt	89 Grenadier Rgt	84 Infantry Rgt	31 Infantry Rgt
76 Infantry Rgt	90 Fusiliers Rgt	86 Fusiliers Rgt	85 Infantry Rgt

Cavalry 16 Dragoon Rgt (3 Sqns)
Artillery 17 Bde: 24 F.A. Rgt, 60 F.A. Rgt

Cavalry 16 Dragoon Rgt (3 Sqns)
Artillery 18 Bde: 9 F.A. Rgt, 45 F.A. Rgt

ABOVE **German Army divisions had an aviation detachment as an integral part of their organisation – a sharp contrast to both British and French practice in which the flying services were ancillaries under independent command. These Bavarian Air Service members pose for the camera just before the start of the last peacetime manoeuvres. The aircraft in the background, an Otto Pusher, was unique to the Bavarian Service. (Author's Collection)**

III RESERVE CORPS
General von Beseler

7TH RESERVE DIVISION

13 Res. Brigade
27 Res. Infantry Rgt
36 Res. Infantry Rgt

14 Res. Brigade
66 Res. Infantry Rgt
72 Res. Infantry Rgt

4 Res. Jaeger Battalion

Cavalry 1 Res. Heavy Cavalry Rgt (3 Sqns)
Artillery 7 Res. F.A. Rgt (6 Batteries)

22ND RESERVE DIVISION

43 Res. Brigade
71 Res. Infantry Rgt
94 Res. Infantry Rgt

44 Res. Brigade
32 Res. Infantry Rgt
82 Res. Infantry Rgt

1 Res. Jaeger Battalion

Cavalry 1 Res. Horse Jaeger Rgt (3 Sqns)
Artillery 22 Res. F.A. Rgt. (6 Batteries)

IX RESERVE CORPS
General von Boehn

17TH RESERVE DIVISION

81 Brigade
162 Infantry Rgt
163 Infantry Rgt

33 Res. Brigade
75 Reserve Rgt
76 Reserve Rgt

Cavalry 6 Res. Hussars Rgt (3 Sqns)
Artillery 17 Res. F.A. Rgt (6 Batteries)

18TH RESERVE DIVISION

53 Reserve Brigade
84 Res. Infantry Rgt
86 Res. Infantry Rgt

36 Reserve Brigade
31 Res. Infantry Rgt
90 Res. Infantry Rgt

9 Res. Jaeger Battalion
Cavalry 7 Res.Hussars Rgt. (3 Sqns)
Artillery 18 Res. F.A. Rgt (6 Batteries)

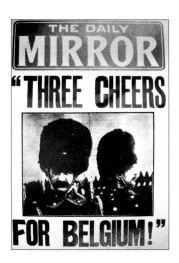

THE DAILY MIRROR
"THREE CHEERS FOR BELGIUM!"

ABOVE **The apparent check to the German advance by the forts which ringed the Belgian town of Liège created great enthusiasm in Britain. A popular song rashly claimed that 'Belgium put the kibosh on the Kaiser' and the *Daily Mirror* echoed the popular feeling of the time. (Author's Collection by courtesy of Mirror Newspapers)**

SECOND ARMY
Generaloberst von Bülow

GUARD CORPS

1ST GUARD DIVISION

1 Guard Brigade	**2 Guard Brigade**
1 Ft. Guard Rgt	2 Ft. Guard Rgt
3 Ft. Guard Rgt	4 Ft. Guard Rgt

Artillery 1st Guard Bde: 1st Gd. Rgt, 3rd Gd. Rgt

2ND GUARD DIVISION

3 Guard Brigade	**4 Guard Brigade**	**5 Guard Brigade**
1 Grenadiers Rgt	2 Grenadiers Rgt	5 Grenadiers Rgt
3 Grenadiers Rgt	4 Grenadiers Rgt	5 Foot Rgt

Artillery 2 Guard Bde: 2 Gd. F.A. Rgt, 4 Gd. F.A. Rgt

VII CORPS
General von Einem

14TH DIVISION

27th Brigade	**79th Brigade**
16 Infantry Rgt	56 Infantry Rgt
53 Infantry Rgt	57 Infantry Rgt

Cavalry 16 Uhlan Rgt (3 Sqns)
Artillery 14 Bde: 7 F.A. Rgt, 43 F.A. Rgt

13TH DIVISION

25th Brigade	**26th Brigade**
13 Infantry Rgt	15 Infantry Rgt
158 Infantry Rgt	55 Infantry Rgt

Cavalry 16 Uhlan Rgt (3 Sqns)
Artillery 13 Bde: 22 F.A. Rgt, 58 F.A. Rgt

X CORPS
General von Emmich

19TH DIVISION

37th Brigade	**38th Brigade**
78 Infantry Rgt	73 Fusiliers
91 Infantry Rgt	74 Infantry Rgt

Cavalry 17 Hussars Rgt (3 Sqns)
Artillery 19 Bde: 26 F.A. Rgt, 62 F.A. Rgt

20TH DIVISION

39th Brigade	**40th Brigade**
79 Infantry Rgt	77 Infantry Rgt
164 Infantry Rgt	92 Infantry Rgt

Cavalry 17 Hussars Rgt (3 Sqns)
Artillery 20th Bde: 10 F.A. Rgt, 46 F.A. Rgt

There was little doubt in Britain that the tiny BEF would rapidly halt the German advance and drive Kaiser Wilhelm's army back to Berlin with its tail between its legs. This postcard appeared within the first weeks of the outbreak of war and at least acknowledges a French presence by including the tricolour! (Author's Collection)

The tiny Belgian Army had little enough with which to fight. This photograph of Belgian troops digging a trench shows a touching naïvety. The Belgian soldiers are wearing a peculiar headgear reminiscent of the American Civil War Hardee hat and are clearly unconcerned about the possible proximity of the enemy! (Author's Collection)

GUARD RESERVE CORPS
General von Gallwitz

3RD GUARD DIVISION

5th Guard Brigade
5 Ft. Rgt
5 Grenadiers Rgt

6th Guard Brigade
Guard Fusiliers
Lehr Rgt

Cavalry Guard Res. Uhlan Rgt
Artillery 5 Guard F.A. Rgt, 6 Guard F.A. Rgt

1ST GUARD RES. DIVISION

1 Guard Res. Brigade
1 Guard Reserve Rgt
2 Guard Reserve Rgt

15th Res. Brigade
64 Reserve Rgt
93 Reserve Rgt

Guard Res. Sniper Battalion

Cavalry Guard Res. Dragoons (3 Sqns)
Artillery 5 Guard Res. F.A. Rgt,
3 Guard Res. F.A. Rgt

VII RESERVE CORPS
General von Zwehl

13TH RESERVE DIVISION

25 Reserve Brigade
13 Res. Infantry Rgt
56 Res. Infantry Rgt

28 Reserve Brigade
39 Res. Infantry Rgt
57 Res. Rgt

7 Res. Jaeger Battalion

Cavalry 5 Res. Hussars Rgt
Artillery 13 Res. F.A. Rgt (6 Batteries)

14TH RESERVE DIVISION

27 Reserve Brigade
16 Res. Infantry Rgt
53 Res. Infantry Rgt

28 Brigade
39 Fusiliers Rgt
159 Infantry Rgt

Cavalry 8 Res. Hussars Rgt (3 Sqns)
Artillery 14 Res. F.A. Rgt (6 Batteries)

X RESERVE CORPS
General von Kirchbach

2ND GUARD RESERVE DIVISION

26 Reserve Brigade
15 Res. Infantry Rgt
55 Res. Infantry Rgt

38 Reserve Brigade
38 Res. Infantry Rgt
91 Res. Infantry Rgt

10 Res. Jager Battalion

Cavalry 2 Res. Uhlan Rgt (3 Sqns)
Artillery 20 Res. F.A. Rgt (6 Batteries)

19TH RESERVE DIVISION

37 Reserve Brigade
73 Res. Infantry Rgt
78 Res. Infantry Rgt

39 Reserve Brigade
74 Rese. Infantry Rgt
92 Res. Infantry Rgt

79 Res. Infantry Rgt (2 Battalions)
10 Res. Jager Battalion

Cavalry 6 Res. Dragoon Rgt (3 Sqns)
Artillery 19 Res. F.A. Rgt (6 Batteries)

25th Landwehr Brigade (later to become part of 25th Landwehr Division)
29th Landwehr Brigade (later to become part of 29th Landwehr Division)
4 Mortar battalions
1 10-cm gun battalion
2 Heavy Coast Mortar Battalions
2 Pionier regiments

World War I has been called the second large war of the Industrial Age, the first being the American Civil War. Mass transportation made it possible to quickly move large numbers of men and vast quantities of munitions and supplies. For Germany, in particular, the railways were an integral part of her war planning and the officers who manned the Railways Directorate of the German General Staff were the best available – it was on them that the smooth running of the whole German war machine depended. (Private Collection)

THIRD ARMY
Lieutenant-General Freiherr von Hausen

XI CORPS

22ND DIVISION		38TH DIVISION	
43 Brigade	**44 Brigade**	**76th Brigade**	**83rd Brigade**
82 Infantry Rgt	32 Infantry Rgt	71 Infantry Rgt	94 Infantry Rgt
83 Infantry Rgt	167 Infantry Rgt	95 Infantry Rgt	96 Infantry Rgt

Cavalry 6 Cuirassier Rgt (3 Sqns)
Artillery 22 Bde: 11 F.A. Rgt, 47 F.A. Rgt

Cavalry 6 Cuirassier Rgt (3 Sqns)
Artillery 38 Bde: 19 Rgt, 55 Rgt

XII (1ST SAXON) CORPS
General d'Elsa

23RD DIVISION		32ND DIVISION	
45 Brigade	**44 Brigade**	**63 Brigade**	**64 Brigade**
100 Grenadiers Rgt	108 Fusiliers Rgt	102 Infantry Rgt	177 Infantry Rgt
101 Grenadiers Rgt	182 Infantry Rgt	103 Infantry Rgt	178 Infantry Rgt
12 Jaeger Battalion			

Cavalry 20 Hussar Rgt
Artillery 23 Bde: 12 F.A. Rgt, 48 F.A. Rgt

Cavalry 18 Hussar Rgt
Artillery 32 Bde: 28 F.A. Rgt, 64 F.A. Rgt

XIX (2ND SAXON) CORPS
General von Laffert

24TH DIVISION

47 Brigade
139 Infantry Rgt
179 Infantry Rgt

48 Brigade
106 Infantry Rgt
107 Infantry Rgt

Cavalry 18 Uhlan Rgt
Artillery 24 Bde: 77 F.A. Rgt, 78 F.A. Rgt

40TH DIVISION

88 Brigade
104 Infantry Rgt
181 Infantry Rgt

89 Brigade
133 Infantry Rgt
134 Infantry Rgt

13 Jaeger Battalion

Cavalry 9 Hussar Rgt
Artillery 40 Bde: 32 Rgt, 68 Rgt

XII (SAXON) RESERVE CORPS
General von Kirchbach

23RD RESERVE DIVISION

45 Reserve Brigade
100 Res. Grenadiers
101 Res. Infantry Rgt

46 Reserve Brigade
102 Res. Infantry Rgt
103 Res. Infantry Rgt

12 Res. Jaeger Battalion

Cavalry Res. Hussar Rgt (3 Sqns)
Artillery 23 Res. F.A. Rgt (9 Batteries)

24TH RESERVE DIVISION

47 Reserve Brigade
104 Res. Infantry Rgt
106 Res. Infantry Rgt

48 Reserve Brigade
107 Res. Infantry Rgt
133 Res. Infantry Rgt

13 Res. Jager Battalion

Cavalry Saxon Reserve Hussar Rgt
Artillery 24 Reserve F.A. Rgt (9 Batteries)

47th Landwehr Brigade (later 47th Landwehr Division)
2 Mortar Battalions
1 Pionier Rgt

I CAVALRY CORPS
Lieutenant-General Freiherr von Richtofen

GUARD CAVALRY DIVISION
5TH CAVALRY DIVISION

II CAVALRY CORPS
Lieutenant-General von der Marwitz

2 CAVALRY DIVISION
4 CAVALRY DIVISION
9 CAVALRY DIVISION

There was no doubt in the mind of the German soldier as to the enemy nor the aim of the invasion – Paris would be occupied in a matter of days!

THE OPPOSING PLANS

GERMANY'S SCHLIEFFEN PLAN

Germany's offensive plan, produced by Count Alfred von Schlieffen, Chief of the General Staff from 1891 to 1906, was a response to the Franco-Russian military pact of 1894 which had created the spectre of a war on two fronts. Germany could anticipate such an event by attacking first, but was not strong enough to combat both countries together. One had to be defeated before the other could be tackled.

Von Schlieffen believed that the greater danger came from France and calculated that it would take the Russians six weeks to launch an offensive. He aimed to repeat the result of the Franco-Prussian War of 1870, when the French Armies were defeated in just 33 days, and the war reached its climax at Sedan, a classic envelopment battle. If the French could be beaten as swiftly again, the German Army could then be sent to the Eastern Front to destroy the Russians.

For the French, the final humiliation of 1870 was the loss of the provinces of Alsace and Lorraine. Their obsession with regaining the lost territory became a vital part of von Schlieffen's thinking. The 150 miles of common frontier with France was between Luxemburg and Switzerland. It was an area of woods, mountains and rivers, with fortresses at Verdun, Toul, Nancy, Epinal and Belfort. Attacks here stood little chance of achieving the necessary swift success.

Von Schlieffen therefore proposed a vast swinging hook through Belgium to France, through Artois and Picardy, bypassing Paris before moving eastward to take the French forts in the rear. Allowing 39 days for the defeat of France, the plan needed an army of five million men, enormous industrial capacity and a first-class railway system subordinated to military need.

In its final form, the plan called for a mere ten divisions to hold Russia in the East; 62 divisions would face France, 54 of them, spread among the First to Fifth Armies, would carry out the assault. The other eight were allocated to the Sixth and Seventh Armies

British mobilisation was equally dependent upon a first-rate rail system allied to a carefully planned scheme for shipping men and munitions across the Channel. Here troops of the 11th Hussars are seen approaching Le Havre on 16 August 1914. (Mons Museum)

on the Franco-German frontier. They would retreat in the face of the anticipated French attack in Alsace and Lorraine and lure their opponents into a trap. As the French dashed forward, they would leave their rear unprotected. In the words of the historian Liddell Hart, the Schlieffen Plan was like a revolving door: 'if a man pressed heavily on one side, the other would swing round and hit him in the back'. It would be another Sedan.

Von Schlieffen wanted 'the right sleeve of the right-hand man to brush the Channel', but after his retirement in 1906, consistent revisions shrivelled the proportionate weight of the right and left wings from six to one, to two to one. The right wing would no longer follow the coast but be well inland. It was an alteration which would eventually lead the German First Army to Mons.

After landing, the British Army moved to Maubeuge, on the left flank of Lanrezac's Fifth French Army. These troops, assembled at a base camp, would shortly start their march north towards the advancing German First and Second Armies. (Mons Museum)

THE FRENCH PLAN XVII AND THE ROLE OF THE BEF

After 1870 French military thinking had concentrated on defence but, in the early 1900s, these ideas became anathema to a fresh generation of officers. At its most basic, the new doctrine asserted that attack was all-important and particularly well suited to the temperament of the French soldier. The concept of 'the massed onslaught at the decisive point' where, irrespective of all else, the surging battalions smashed through an enemy, recalled the days of glory of the First Empire. Bonaparte's battles against the Austrians were cited approvingly; the Peninsula and Waterloo were ignored.

THE CONCENTRATION OF THE ARMIES – AUGUST 1914

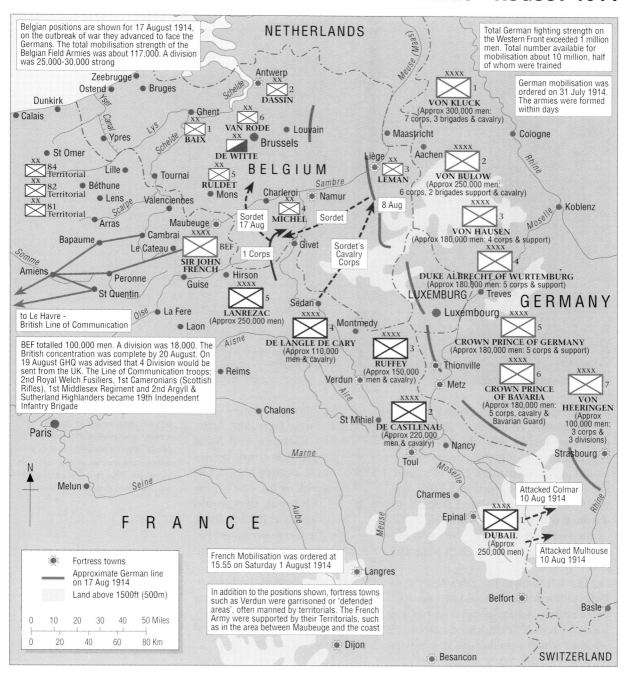

Belgian positions are shown for 17 August 1914, on the outbreak of war they advanced to face the Germans. The total mobilisation strength of the Belgian Field Armies was about 117,000. A division was 25,000-30,000 strong

NETHERLANDS

Total German fighting strength on the Western Front exceeded 1 million men. Total number available for mobilisation about 10 million, half of whom were trained

German mobilisation was ordered on 31 July 1914. The armies were formed within days

Zeebrugge
Ostend • Bruges
Dunkirk
Calais
Antwerp
XX 2
DASSIN
Ghent
XX 6
VAN RODE
Louvain
Brussels
XX
DE WITTE
Maastricht
Aachen
Cologne

XXXX 1
VON KLUCK
(Approx 300,000 men:
7 corps, 3 brigades & cavalry)

XXXX 2
VON BULOW
(Approx 250,000 men:
6 corps, 2 brigades support & cavalry)

Rhine

St Omer
Lille
Ypres
XX 84 Territorial
XX 82 Territorial
XX 81 Territorial
Béthune
Lens
Arras
Tournai
Valenciennes
Scarpe
Mons
XX 1 BAIX
XX 5 RULDET
Charleroi
XX 4 MICHEL
Namur
Sambre
Liège
XX 3 LEMAN

8 Aug

XXXX 3
VON HAUSEN
(Approx 180,000 men: 4 corps & support)

Moselle
Koblenz

Bapaume
Amiens
Le Cateau
Cambrai
Maubeuge
XXXX BEF
SIR JOHN FRENCH
Somme
Sordet 17 Aug
1 Corps
Givet
Sordet
Sordet's Cavalry Corps

XXXX 4
DUKE ALBRECHT OF WURTEMBURG
(Approx 180,000 men: 5 corps & support)
LUXEMBURG
Treves
GERMANY

Peronne
St Quentin
Hirson
Guise
XXXX 5
LANREZAC
(Approx 250,000 men)
Sedan
Luxembourg

to Le Havre -
British Line of Communication
Oise
La Fere
Laon
Aisne
XXXX 4
DE LANGLE DE CARY
(Approx 110,000 men & cavalry)
Montmedy

XXXX 3
RUFFEY
(Approx 150,000 men & cavalry)
Verdun
Thionville
Metz

XXXX 5
CROWN PRINCE OF GERMANY
(Approx 180,000 men: 5 corps & support)

BEF totalled 100,000 men. A division was 18,000. The British concentration was complete by 20 August. On 19 August GHQ was advised that 4 Division would be sent from the UK. The Line of Communication troops; 2nd Royal Welch Fusiliers, 1st Cameronians (Scottish Rifles), 1st Middlesex Regiment and 2nd Argyll & Sutherland Highlanders became 19th Independent Infantry Brigade

Reims
Chalons
St Mihiel
XXXX 2
DE CASTLENAU
(Approx 220,000 men & cavalry)
Nancy

XXXX 6
CROWN PRINCE OF BAVARIA
(Approx 180,000 men: 5 corps, cavalry & Bavarian Guard)

XXXX 7
VON HEERINGEN
(Approx 100,000 men: 3 corps & 3 divisions)

Paris
Marne
Toul
Moselle
Strasbourg

N

Melun
Seine
Aube
Charmes
Epinal
XXXX 1
DUBAIL
(Approx 250,000 men)
Attacked Colmar 10 Aug 1914

FRANCE
Meuse

Attacked Mulhouse 10 Aug 1914

Fortress towns
Approximate German line on 17 Aug 1914
Land above 1500ft (500m)

French Mobilisation was ordered at 15.55 on Saturday 1 August 1914

Langres

Belfort
Basle

0 10 20 30 40 50 Miles
0 20 40 60 80 Km

In addition to the positions shown, fortress towns such as Verdun were garrisoned or 'defended areas', often manned by territorials. The French Army were supported by their Territorials, such as in the area between Maubeuge and the coast

Dijon

Besancon
SWITZERLAND

The new discipline of the offensive reached its zenith with Plan XVII issued in February 1914. It opened with a startling lack of appreciation of German intentions, as well as a blithe disregard of French Intelligence assessments: 'From a careful study of information obtained,' it began, 'it is probable that a great part of the German forces will be concentrated on the common frontier.' After this unpromising start, Plan XVII continued: 'Whatever the circumstances, it is the C-in-C's intention to

27

advance with all forces united to the attack of the German Armies.'

Impressive results were anticipated. On the extreme right, the Army of Alsace would take the area where the French, German and Swiss borders met; along the common frontier, the First and Second Armies would advance through Lorraine and the Saarland to occupy Mainz. On the left wing, the Third and Fifth Armies would attack to the east unless the Germans had violated Belgian neutrality. In this event, they would advance through Luxemburg and the Ardennes to strike at the left flank of the German Army. Any invasion of Belgium by the Germans would be, in the opinion of the French planners, limited to a small area east of the River Meuse.

The left flank of the Fifth Army would be at Hirson, close to the Franco-Belgian border, and would be extended by the arrival of the BEF. Between them and the Channel ports was a 100-mile gap garrisoned by three poorly trained French Territorial divisions. The BEF would be part of a general advance which would crush the unprotected German right flank.

The Fourth Army, which was largely made up of Reserve divisions, would be ordered forward to occupy Berlin once the other armies had defeated the enemy.

Details of reserves and timetables were scant, but it was confidently assumed that nothing could go wrong. The whirlwind offensive would completely dislocate German plans. Plan XVII further ignored any possibility of a major German attack through Belgium and that meant that there would not be one. Plan XVII could not be wrong. It was a theory that would cost the French Army more than 250,000 casualties in August 1914.

The reality was this – German cavalry advancing in August 1914 – a surreptitious photograph. These troops were the actual spearpoint of the German advance. This is a photograph of an invasion. (Private Collection)

THE ARRIVAL OF THE BEF

The first British soldiers arrived at Mons on 21 August. They were patrols from the 9th Lancers and 18th Hussars, probing northward for signs of the enemy. Local residents and refugees spoke of the roads south of Brussels being filled with marching Germans.

The next morning, north of Mons at Casteau, at about 7am, Cpl. Drummer Thomas of 'C' Squadron of the 4th Dragoon Guards fired at a mounted figure and claimed a hit. Whether it was or not, a British Army bandsman had fired the first British shot in the First World War. His target was probably from the 4th Cuirassiers, for an hour later four or five suspicious troopers from that unit came warily along the road towards the eager British.

Two troops of dragoons rode to engage them. The outnumbered cuirassiers retreated and the dragoons gave chase. The Germans reached their squadron which retreated further. After a hot pursuit over another two miles, the dragoons caught the enemy and in the skirmish which followed about 15 Germans were killed and eight taken prisoner.

Later that day, the Royal Scots Greys, fighting a dismounted action, persuaded a strong German force from the 13th Division of the VII Corps and part of Second Army's I Cavalry Corps to retreat under the impression they were fighting a full brigade. The 16th Lancers met two companies of

Although aircraft were being used for reconnaissance, all the combatant armies relied on their cavalry to probe ahead of the main infantry force and act as scouts. This postcard, entitled 'Uhlans In The Vanguard!', shows a cavalry patrol asking questions from a helpful Belgian civilian – it came as a rude shock to Kaiser Wilhelm's High Command that the Belgians actually resisted the German advance. (Michael Solka)

RIGHT **Their armies' advance into France and Belgium was presented as an unrelieved triumphal progress in the German newspapers of the time. Unlike the British, the German Army had its own photographers who were soon supplying a stream of pictures to the home front to keep up civilian morale. In this shot a typical German infantryman 'snatches a moment during the advance to write a personal postcard home to his loved ones'. (Private Collection)**

Jaegers in the open and charged them with the lance. A number of the enemy were speared for the loss of a handful of British troopers.

The cavalry reports went back to GHQ, their conclusions being that strong German forces were advancing on Mons. Twelve reconnaissance missions made by the infant Royal Flying Corps also reported the presence of large masses of enemy troops. The information made little impact at GHQ, as French and his staff were concentrating on plans for a general offensive.

It had been a busy time for the BEF since mobilisation on 4 August. The advance parties left for France on 7 August, and the main elements began their journey on the 12th. Southampton was the main embarkation port for the troops, except for those stationed in Ireland, who left from Dublin, Cork and Belfast. Motor transport (the British Army was the most mechanised in Europe) and petrol left from Avonmouth and Liverpool, stores and supplies were despatched from Newhaven. Ports and railways were put to a severe test; 80 trains were required to move a division, and 1,800 special trains were needed during the five days it took to get the BEF and its supplies to the embarkation points. On the busiest day, there were 137 sea crossings as the troop ships and transports laboured back and forth. By the evening of 17 August, the vast majority of the BEF had disembarked at Le Havre, Rouen and Boulogne.

They received a rapturous welcome and were deluged with flowers and kisses, wine and food. Cap badges and shoulder titles were handed over to enthusiastic admirers. An infantry officer, marching through the cheering crowds on the trek to Maubeuge, recalled years later that 'I felt like a king among men'.

Since 4 August, the German Army had ploughed across Belgium. Liège was captured on 16 August, and von Kluck's First Army was swinging round to the west and advancing towards the French frontier. Von Bulow's Second Army was south of Liège and the Third Army under Gen. Hausen was moving through the Ardennes. Von Moltke, the Chief of the German General Staff, in order to control the pace and alignment of the right, decided to form the three armies into an Army Group under the control of von Bulow. Von Kluck was furious, his reaction simple. He merely ignored all orders from his nominal superior.

The Germans entered Brussels on 20 August, and on the same day, Sir John French issued Operation Order No 5 which instructed the BEF 'to march north'. This was in accordance with the rapidly crumbling Plan XVII, which required Lanrezac, commander of the French Fifth Army of which the BEF was now an appendage, to move into Belgian territory east of the River Meuse if the Germans breached Belgian neutrality. It was thought the joint force would meet only light opposition.

THE ADVANCE ON MONS – AUGUST 1914

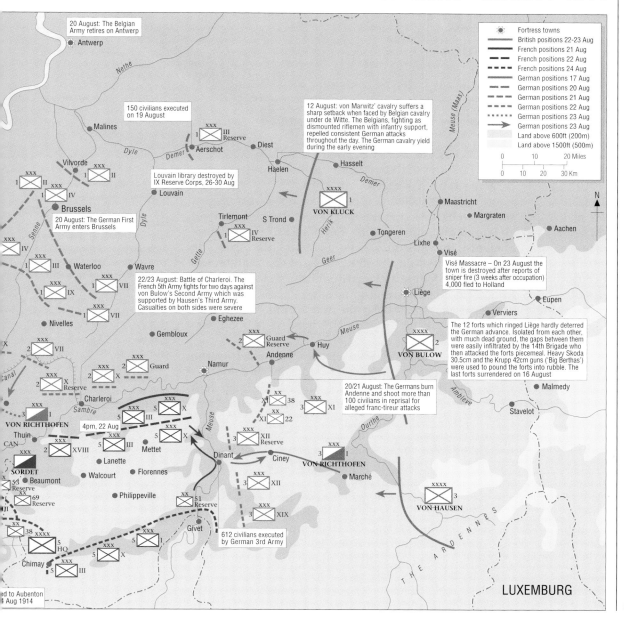

Lanrezac's change of plan

In fact, Lanrezac was facing 700,000 men in the three German armies. He had already started to have second thoughts about the wisdom of an offensive. As time passed and more reports came in, he became more cautious. By 21 August, he was sure. The French Fifth Army, he reasoned, held the high ground on the south bank of the Sambre, was protected on the right by the Meuse and was thus in a first class defensive position. It would be madness to leave it to meet an enemy who was in great strength. Therefore, he would delay the attack until the time was opportune. The BEF, unaware of Lanrezac's change of opinion, was marching confidently northwards.

Lanrezac was right. The planned advance would neatly deliver the Fifth Army into a salient where it could be destroyed from three sides.

Matters got worse. On the afternoon of 21 August, the 'excellent defences' on the Sambre were breached by the German Second Army. Despite talk of counterattacking the next day, Lanrezac decided on retreat. His concern was to save his Army. Intact, it could still fight; destroyed or captured, the route to Paris was wide open. The Fifth Army, along with the Fourth Army on its right, began to fall back the next day under constant pressure from the Germans.

Generaloberst von Kluck, meanwhile, had his own problems. He was concerned about his right flank. Under the impression that the BEF had probably landed at Ostend, Dunkirk and Calais, he was anxious to move towards the coast to intercept any threat from the Channel ports. Von Bulow, however, disagreed. Living up to his reputation as a cautious commander who believed in mutual support, he was more concerned about the growing gap between the First and Second Armies, and ordered von Kluck to turn south-west in case 'the First Army might get too far away

The BEF was greeted with enormous enthusiasm by the French population. Many British troops lost cap badges and shoulder titles in response to urgent appeals for souvenirs. This picture, taken by a press photographer, emphasises the high level of mechanisation of the British Army compared to its Continental rivals. Thanks to the 'Subsidy Scheme' under which commercial companies received from the War Office part of the cost of buying and operating approved lorries and vans in return for yielding up the transport if needed in time of war, the British Army could claim to be one of the most highly mechanised in the world. Many of the vehicles initially went to France in their civilian livery – a point much appreciated by the aircrew of 5 Squadron, Royal Flying Corps, who used their scarlet and gold painted lorry (from the makers of HP Sauce) as a homing device during the constant moves of the Advance to Mons and the subsequent Retreat! (Private Collection)

Belgian cyclist troops 'advancing towards the enemy' if the original caption is to be believed. Interestingly, in the original photograph a car on the left of the picture appears to be filled with British officers – presumably retreating from the enemy! (Author's Collection)

and not be able to support the Second Army'. Von Kluck protested, but Supreme Headquarters intervened to support von Bulow. Von Kluck fumed but had to conform.

So it was that a Royal Flying Corps crew reported on Saturday 22 August that they had seen a huge column of enemy troops marching towards the BEF. It was von Kluck's II Corps and they were on their way to Mons.

It was Lt. Spears, the British liaison officer at Lanrezac's headquarters, who saved the BEF from extinction. Learning on the Saturday afternoon of Lanrezac's decision to retreat, as well as getting some indication of the size of the German assault, he set off for GHQ along roads jammed with transport and refugees. It took him four hours. He arrived at eight o'clock in the evening to discover the staff busy with final arrangements for continuing the advance. Spears made his report to Sir John French and the planning was abruptly discontinued. New instructions were issued to halt the advance and prepare for battle.

There was to be a final surprising request. As the orders went out to the BEF to hold its ground, one of Lanrezac's staff officers arrived. Lanrezac wanted the BEF to swing to the east and attack von Bulow's Second Army to take pressure off the Fifth Army. This would have exposed the flank of the BEF to the full weight of von Kluck's assault. As it was, Sir John French agreed to hold his existing position for 24 hours.

THE BATTLE OF MONS

The main body of the BEF had already reached Mons. II Corps spread out along the line of the Mons-Condé Canal which ran directly westwards from the town. I Corps occupied the salient to the east of Mons. By nightfall the BEF was nine miles ahead of Lanrezac's retreating Fifth Army, with a ten mile gap on the right between the British and French. On the left, there was intermittent contact with the 84th French Territorial Division, and Allenby's Cavalry Corps was ordered across to support the left.

The last elements of the BEF did not reach Mons until 3am on 23 August after a long and gruelling three days' march. 'We were saddled with pack and equipment weighing nearly eighty pounds and our khaki uniforms, flannel shirts, and thick woollen pants, fit for an Arctic climate, added to our discomfort in the sweltering heat,' one Reservist recalled. New boots, the heat, and the strain of continual marching along cobbled roads brought many soldiers to a state of collapse.

Mons was the centre of the Belgian coal mining area. A string of dreary villages, interspersed with slag heaps, factories and coal tips, ran along the 16 mile length of the canal. Eighteen bridges crossed it. No more than two metres deep, and with a width of about 20 metres, the canal was hardly an obstacle. The view to the north, from which the attack would come, was obscured by grim terraces of cottages, factories and slag heaps. The higher ground was fringed with trees which made both movement and vision difficult for the defenders.

Behind the cavalry trudged the indomitable infantry, suffering badly in the August heat. Germans, French, Belgians and British alike recall sweltering August conditions. This group of British senior NCOs were caught by the camera in northern France just before the move into Belgium. (Mons Museum)

Countering the Allied claims of 'Hun atrocities' in Belgium and France rapidly became a priority for the German propaganda service. There is little doubt that atrocities occurred – von Moltke, the German Commander-in-Chief, expressed his own shock at the brutal behaviour reported to him. Favourable stories and photographs of German activities were supplied to the press in neutral countries – German soldiers were forever rescuing Belgian children from flooded streams, swirling mill ponds and deep canals – together with stories attempting to justify repressive action on the part of the German authorities. The US Ambassador to Belgium recalled that the continual German justifications made him feel that the burgemeesters or mayors of Belgian towns had bred a special race of children, so often was the reason advanced for a particular atrocity that the son or daughter of a local burgemeester had attacked an innocent or unarmed German soldier. This picture was one of a series purporting to show the warm welcome offered to the occupiers by the Belgians. (Author's Collection)

The BEF dug in, borrowing picks and shovels from the local civilians to eke out their own supply. Both Haig and Smith-Dorrien were concerned about their ability to hold their positions. II Corps, in particular, with some 36,000 men in total, had the almost impossible job of defending a 21 mile long front line running from the bridge at Le Petit Crépin in the west to the bridge at Obourg in the east. The canal curved round the town of Mons to join the River Sambre and this created a salient which included the road and railway bridges into Mons itself. On the right of Smith-Dorrien's position, I Corps faced east so that the whole length of the British position looked a little like a walking stick with a curved handle.

Sensibly and conventionally enough, the British infantry were concentrated to deny the bridges to the advancing foe. Outposts were deployed on the northern side of the canal to cover the approaches to the bridges. The soldiers scraped holes where they could, erected barricades from anything they could find, concealed themselves wherever possible and waited for morning.

Smith-Dorrien had commanded II Corps for only a day. He had been sent hastily from England to replace Sir James Grierson who had died suddenly on 17 August. Smith-Dorrien had enjoyed a less than harmonious interview with Sir John French, who had instructed him to give battle along the line of the canal. Smith-Dorrien had asked if it was an offensive or a defensive operation and received the not altogether encouraging response that he should obey orders.

Smith-Dorrien's doubts were not eased during a personal visit by Sir John French early in the morning of 23 August. With one of those contradictory instructions which baffled those who served under him, he told Haig, Allenby and Smith-Dorrien 'to be prepared to move forward, or to fight where they were', and to ready the bridges across the canal for demolition. He further assured his corps commanders that 'little more than one, or two, enemy corps with perhaps a cavalry division' were

The German army entered Brussels on the 20th August, 1914. Long horse-drawn columns of guns and transports, interspersed with marching infantry, relentlessly singing themselves hoarse as they passed through the Belgian capital, brought home to watching civilians the awesome power that they faced. It took three days and nights for the Germans to go through Brussels and, as one witness dolefully recalled, it was the non-stop singing of marching songs that was the worst part of it. (Private Collection)

LEFT Reports of clashes between German and British cavalry led to a rash of popular pictures in both countries; cavalry actions were dashing and romantic, evoking past eras of combat. This illustration, produced early in the war, shows a determined German cuirassier spearing a terrified British opponent. (Michael Solka)

advancing on the BEF. This optimistic assessment was totally at variance with the reports of both the British and French Intelligence staff. They estimated that a minimum of three German Army corps were approaching Mons.

Smith-Dorrien expressed his worry about his position along the canal. He had already reconnoitred a new defence line two miles south of the canal which eliminated the town of Mons and the salient. He told French that he was preparing orders for his troops to retire to this line if they were in danger of being cut off by the advancing Germans. Smith-Dorrien was later to claim that Sir John had agreed with his views and approved his plans, a conclusion which the Commander-in-Chief subsequently denied. Sir John then departed for Valenciennes, leaving his army to fight its first battle of the war. GHQ was to issue no further written orders until the morning of 24 August and Sir John French's contact with his army became extremely haphazard.

The opening shots

Even as the commanders talked, the first skirmishes had started. In a drizzling, misty dawn, the Germans began a short bombardment which caused about 20 casualties, and the 4th Middlesex opened fire on a German cavalry patrol pushing forward to the salient east of Mons. Lt. von Arnim of the Husaren Regiment Nr. 1 was taken prisoner. He was shot through the knee and would walk with a limp for the rest of his days. As the sun came out, clearing the mist and rain, more German cavalry were seen along the whole length of the line. They were the advance guard of the 3rd, the 9th and the 2nd Cavalry Corps of the First Army.

Von Kluck, still smarting under his changed orders, had little idea of the location of the BEF. His troops stumbled upon British forces by chance. Instead of co-ordinated attacks, there were thus a series of small-scale actions. If von Kluck had concentrated the full weight of the four

THE BATTLE OF MONS
23 AUGUST 1914

The BEF's first encounter with von Kluck's First Army. Along a line approximately nine miles long, nine and a half British battalions hold four German Divisions at bay for most of the day.

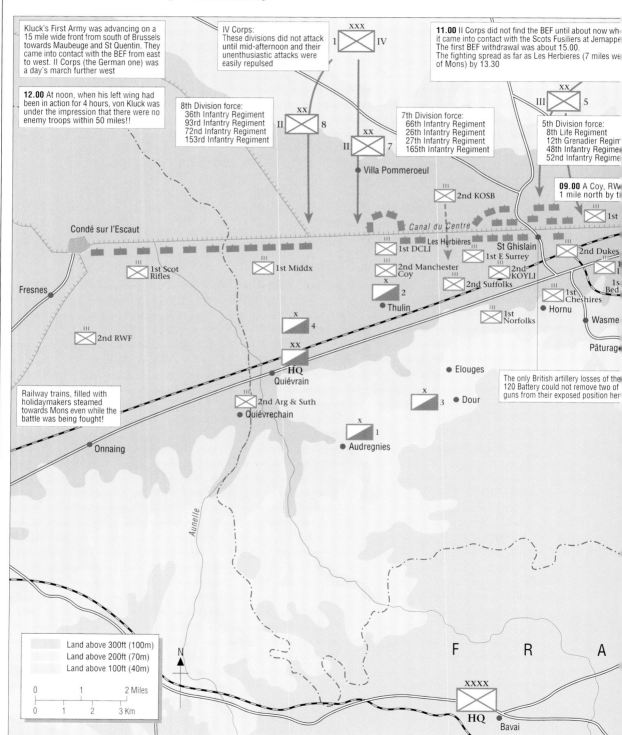

Kluck's First Army was advancing on a 15 mile wide front from south of Brussels towards Maubeuge and St Quentin. They came into contact with the BEF from east to west. II Corps (the German one) was a day's march further west

12.00 At noon, when his left wing had been in action for 4 hours, von Kluck was under the impression that there were no enemy troops within 50 miles!!

IV Corps: These divisions did not attack until mid-afternoon and their unenthusiastic attacks were easily repulsed

11.00 II Corps did not find the BEF until about now wh it came into contact with the Scots Fusiliers at Jemappe The first BEF withdrawal was about 15.00.
The fighting spread as far as Les Herbieres (7 miles we of Mons) by 13.30

8th Division force:
36th Infantry Regiment
93rd Infantry Regiment
72nd Infantry Regiment
153rd Infantry Regiment

7th Division force:
66th Infantry Regiment
26th Infantry Regiment
27th Infantry Regiment
165th Infantry Regiment

5th Division force:
8th Life Regiment
12th Grenadier Regim
48th Infantry Regime
52nd Infantry Regime

09.00 A Coy, RW
1 mile north by t

Villa Pommeroeul

2nd KOSB

Canal du Centre

Conde sur l'Escaut

1st DCLI

Les Herbières

St Ghislain

1st E Surrey

2nd Dukes

1st Scot Rifles

1st Middx

2nd Manchester Coy

2nd KOYLI

2 Thulin

2nd Suffolks

1st Cheshires

1st Bed

Fresnes

Hornu

Wasme

Pâturag

2nd RWF

4

1st Norfolks

Elouges

The only British artillery losses of the 120 Battery could not remove two of guns from their exposed position her

HQ
Quiévrain

3 Dour

Railway trains, filled with holidaymakers steamed towards Mons even while the battle was being fought!

2nd Arg & Suth

Quiévrechain

1

Onnaing

Audregnies

Aunelle

Land above 300ft (100m)
Land above 200ft (70m)
Land above 100ft (40m)

0   1   2 Miles
0 1 2 3 Km

N

F   R   A

HQ
Bavai

Army Corps at his disposal upon the BEF, history would have been very different. As it was, he believed that only cavalry were in front of him, that the main BEF was still somewhere to the south, and allowed the action to develop piecemeal.

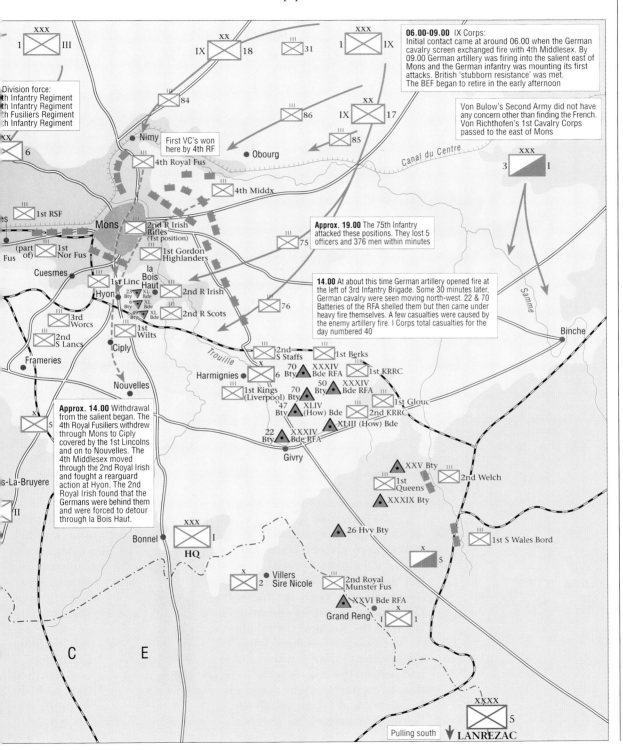

06.00-09.00 IX Corps:
Initial contact came at around 06.00 when the German cavalry screen exchanged fire with 4th Middlesex. By 09.00 German artillery was firing into the salient east of Mons and the German infantry was mounting its first attacks. British 'stubborn resistance' was met.
The BEF began to retire in the early afternoon

Von Bulow's Second Army did not have any concern other than finding the French. Von Richthofen's 1st Cavalry Corps passed to the east of Mons

Division force:
th Infantry Regiment
th Infantry Regiment
th Fusiliers Regiment
th Infantry Regiment

First VC's won here by 4th RF

Nimy

4th Royal Fus

Obourg

Canal du Centre

4th Middx

1st RSF

Mons

2nd R Irish Rifles (1st position)

(part of) 1st Nor Fus

Cuesmes

1st Gordon Highlanders

la Bois Haut

1st Linc

2³rd Bty XL Bde
6th Bty XL Bde
49th Bty XL Bde

2nd R Irish

Hyon

Approx. 19.00 The 75th Infantry attacked these positions. They lost 5 officers and 376 men within minutes

75

14.00 At about this time German artillery opened fire at the left of 3rd Infantry Brigade. Some 30 minutes later, German cavalry were seen moving north-west. 22 & 70 Batteries of the RFA shelled them but then came under heavy fire themselves. A few casualties were caused by the enemy artillery fire. I Corps total casualties for the day numbered 40

2nd R Scots

76

Samme

Binche

3rd Worcs

1st Wilts

2nd S Lancs

Ciply

Frameries

Nouvelles

2nd S Staffs

1st Berks

70 Bty

XXXIV Bde RFA

1st KRRC

Harmignies

1st Kings (Liverpool)

70 Bty

50 Bty

XXXIV Bde RFA

1st Glouc

47 Bty

XLIV (How) Bde

2nd KRRC

Approx. 14.00 Withdrawal from the salient began. The 4th Royal Fusiliers withdrew through Mons to Ciply covered by the 1st Lincolns and on to Nouvelles. The 4th Middlesex moved through the 2nd Royal Irish and fought a rearguard action at Hyon. The 2nd Royal Irish found that the Germans were behind them and were forced to detour through la Bois Haut.

22 Bty

XXXIV Bde RFA

XLIII (How) Bde

Givry

5

XXV Bty

1st Queens

2nd Welch

XXXIX Bty

26 Hvy Bty

1st S Wales Bord

Bonnel

I

HQ

5

Villers Sire Nicole

2

2nd Royal Munster Fus

XXVI Bde RFA

Grand Reng

I

1

C

E

3

I

Pulling south

LANREZAC

5

The main Belgian field army retreated to Antwerp on 20 August. As the Germans occupied Brussels, the Belgians prepared their defences. Optimism was high. This detachment of Belgian infantry demonstrates exactly how they would defend an Antwerp canal against the invader. (Author's Collection)

At about 9am, the German 9th Corps artillery once more opened fire on the salient on the British right .The bombardment was followed by an assault from the 18th Infantry Division, pushing forward between Obourg and Nimy against the 4th Middlesex and the 4th Royal Fusiliers. Eight battalions attacked four companies. The German soldiers approached in a solidly packed mass of close columns and were met by a hail of fire from the entrenched British infantry.

'They went down like a regular lot of Charlie Chaplins,' one British soldier wrote to his wife, 'every bullet hitting home, sometimes taking two men at a time.' Column after column advanced to be met by the same withering fire. Finally, the German attack shivered to a halt and the survivors retreated to the cover of the tree line. Desultory artillery fire continued and after 30 minutes, a new attack was launched.

This time, the Germans came in extended order over a wider frontage; they were joined by the infantry of the 17th Division, and their attacks were pressed home with great courage. The Middlesex, in the east of the salient, suffered under a continuous artillery bombardment, but the infantry attacks were thrown back with heavy German losses. Eventually, the German troops began to operate in smaller groups. Determined parties of enemy infantry managed to cross the canal and infiltrate the flanks of the Middlesex position.

The situation became confused and communication a problem as the shells rained down, but the 'stubborn resistance' which Smith-Dorrien had pressed upon his brigade commanders continued. By mid-morning, despite support from the machine gun section of the 2nd Royal Irish, the Middlesex had begun to fall back, and shortly after midday they were fighting desperately to prevent the German assault from encircling them.

Defence of la Bois Haut

On their right, the 1st Gordons and 2nd Royal Scots, dug in on higher ground at la Bois Haut, were resisting stubbornly as the 17th Division tried to turn the British flank. From this higher ground, the British artillery had both good observation and fields of fire. The German infantry was caught in the open by the gunners of 6, 23 and 49 batteries and suffered heavily from the hail of shrapnel with which they were showered.

The salient was being assaulted on three sides and British losses rose steadily. As the officers were killed or wounded, the individual initiative

British cavalry entered Mons on 21 August 1914. This photograph, taken by a French liaison officer, shows a patrol on its way forward into Belgium on the 20th August. (Mons Museum)

These troopers of the 9th Lancers entering Mons on the 21 August 1914, were the first British soldiers to reach the town. (Mons Museum)

ATTACK OF THE GERMAN 18TH DIVISION AT MONS, 23 AUGUST 1913
Following a bombardment by the German 9th Artillery Corps at about 09.00 the German 18th Division launched an assault against the 4th Middlesex and the 4th Royal Fusiliers between Obourg and Nimy. Eight battalions attacked four companies in close column formation and were cut down in a hail of fire from the British.

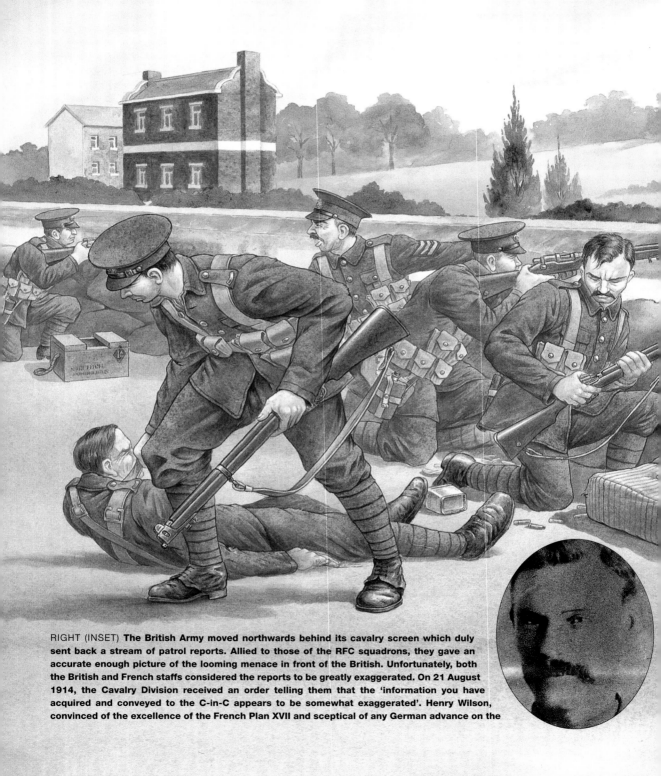

RIGHT (INSET) **The British Army moved northwards behind its cavalry screen which duly sent back a stream of patrol reports. Allied to those of the RFC squadrons, they gave an accurate enough picture of the looming menace in front of the British. Unfortunately, both the British and French staffs considered the reports to be greatly exaggerated. On 21 August 1914, the Cavalry Division received an order telling them that the 'information you have acquired and conveyed to the C-in-C appears to be somewhat exaggerated'. Henry Wilson, convinced of the excellence of the French Plan XVII and sceptical of any German advance on the**

right, was the signatory. It was, not surprisingly, a cavalryman who fired the first British shot of the First World War, the first shot fired in anger on the Continent since the Battle of Waterloo. At Casteau, just north of Mons, Corporal Drummer Thomas of the 4th Dragoon Guards fired at a distant German cavalryman at about 7am on 22nd August 1914. He was forever convinced that he had hit his man. (Mons Museum)

Two British 18th Hussars question members of the local populace at Mons on 21 August 1914. Note the sun hood worn by one of the riders and the fringed tassels over the horses' eyes to keep away flies. (Mons Museum)

of the lower ranks became a vital ingredient of the resistance. By noon, German troops were over the canal in reasonable strength and the enemy artillery was making life extremely unpleasant for the British infantry. The position of the 4th Middlesex was rapidly becoming untenable, and the Royal Irish Regiment, ordered up to support them, found their task complicated by the attentions of the German guns. A German cavalry attack was beaten back by the Irish machine gunners but the enemy's artillery eventually zeroed in and caused severe casualties.

The withdrawal from the salient began at about 2pm. The Royal Fusiliers retired slowly, stubbornly, and reluctantly from the bridges, a task made more difficult because they were in full view of the enemy. At Nimy, Lt. Maurice Dease, the machine gun officer of the Royal Fusiliers, held back two battalions of German infantry as they tried to capture the bridge. Although wounded time and again, Dease fought until he died. He was awarded a posthumous Victoria Cross. It was the first of 628 to be awarded during the First World War. Pte. Sidney Godley, also of the machine gun section, won the second. Remaining on the bridge to cover the withdrawal of the Fusiliers late in the afternoon, already badly wounded, he held his position until everyone else had got away. As a final gesture, he dismantled his machine gun and threw the pieces into the canal. He then crawled back to the main road where he was found by two Belgian civilians and taken to hospital in Mons.

The Fusiliers withdrew through Mons itself and then to Ciply and Nouvelles to the south of the town. Their retreat was covered by the 1st Lincolns who had set up barricades through which the exhausted survivors of the day's fighting passed. The enemy showed no inclination to pursue.

In the remainder of the salient, the fighting became increasingly bitter as the afternoon wore on. The Germans tried to outflank their opponents

RIGHT **Two British cavalrymen and their French interpreter on the Canal du Centre on 21 August 1914. This very poor photograph is nonetheless an interesting moment frozen in time. (Mons Museum)**

BELOW **The Grand-Place at Mons – soldiers of 'A' Company of the 4th Royal Fusiliers, part of the 7th Brigade of 3 Division in Smith-Dorrien's II Corps, shown at rest on the afternoon of 22 August, 1914. From this position today, the facade is virtually unchanged. By the next morning, these soldiers had moved on to Nimy, some 7 kilometres to the north, where they fought off the full weight of the 18th Division of von Kluck's IX Corps. Note the Belgian civilians mixing with the troops. (Mons Museum)**

RIGHT **The 4th Battalion of the Royal Fusiliers won the first two Victoria Crosses of the war. The first to go to a private soldier was that awarded to Private Sidney Godley (see text). Godley was badly wounded in the action defending the bridge at Nimy and was captured when the Germans occupied Mons. His picture, appearing in the papers when his award of the VC was announced, is reputed to have provided Bruce Bairnsfather with the likeness for 'Old Bill'. Certainly, a photograph of Godley in civilian clothes, taken at a subsequent Buckingham Palace reception for Victoria Cross holders, shows a stocky and cheerfully pugnacious figure who could well pass for Bairnsfather's creation. (Imperial War Museum)**

by moving forward to Hyon. This caused problems for the 4th Middlesex and the Royal Irish as they pulled back. The Middlesex, having moved through the Royal Irish, fought a desperate rearguard action on the outskirts of Hyon itself; as the Royal Irish, in their turn, started their withdrawal, they found the Germans behind them and were forced to detour through la Bois Haut.

The battle for the canal

West of the salient, along the line of the canal, the battle had taken longer to develop. The 6th Division of III Corps came upon the British positions at Mariette three miles west of Mons at about 11am. Marching down the road in close column of fours, they were sent reeling sharply backwards by the concentrated fire of the 1st Northumberlands. The Germans tried again, this time being ambushed against a barricade and a wire entanglement. There was a lull while two German field guns were brought up to demolish the Northumberlands' defences; the Fusiliers were then astounded to see a group of Belgian schoolgirls coming down the road towards them.

The enemy, taking advantage of the fact that the British were holding their fire in the face of civilians, rushed forward, and the Northumberland outposts were forced to withdraw across the canal. Whether this was a deliberate ploy by the German attackers or a simple case of civilians being caught up in the fighting is now impossible to determine.

Still further west, more assaults by 6th Division against the bridge at Jemappes were severely punished by the 1st Royal Scots. Again, the Germans attempted to counter the threat by bringing up artillery, but the German field gunners were firing blind. Casualties among the scattered British troops were light and at noon both the Northumberlands and the Royal Scots were still comfortably fending off any attempt to take their bridges.

At St Ghislaine, to the left of the 1st Royal Scots, the 1st Royal West Kents were faced by the 12th Brandenburg Grenadiers of the 5th Division. Amazed British soldiers watched as the German troops

THE BRIDGE AT NIMY 23 AUGUST 1914

To help cover the retreat from the salient Lieutenant Maurice Dease held back two battalions of German infantry attempting to capture the bridge. Repeatedly wounded he fought until he died. Private Sidney Godley took over and remained until everybody had escaped. Although badly wounded he managed to dismantle the gun and throw it into the canal as a final gesture before crawling to the road where he was found by two civilians who took him to hospital. Both soldiers were awarded the Victoria Cross.

advanced, firing from the hip. It was, one considered, 'like watching a military tattoo', but it was also remarkably ineffective, the bullets flying high above Kentish heads. The British battalion had advanced north of the canal and occupied a glass factory. From its cover, they massacred the first attacks without loss to themselves. Faced with increasing odds as the Brandenburg Grenadiers were reinforced, the Kents slipped away as dusk came and took up new positions on the embankment. The final German attacks were stopped some 300 yards north of the canal, great havoc being wrought by four guns of 120 Battery of the Royal Field Artillery which was on the canal towpath.

Like many survivors of the German regiments that tangled with the BEF that day, the Brandenburgers believed the deadly 'mad minute' concentrated rifle fire of the British was the work of machine gunners. It was an understandable mistake; 700 concealed infantry-men, each firing once every four seconds, not only make a lot of noise. They cause many casualties. The vast majority of the attackers had never been under fire before, and the sheer power of the defence was an enormous shock to them.

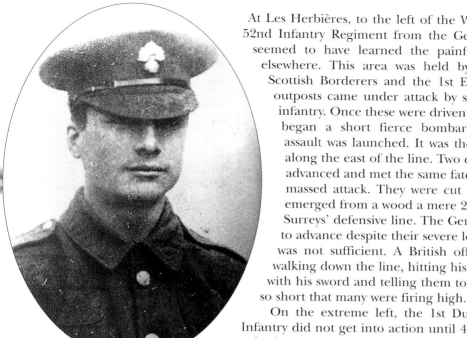

At Les Herbières, to the left of the West Kents' position, the 52nd Infantry Regiment from the German III Corps at first seemed to have learned the painful lesson being taught elsewhere. This area was held by the 2nd King's Own Scottish Borderers and the 1st East Surreys. The KOSB outposts came under attack by small parties of German infantry. Once these were driven in, the German artillery began a short fierce bombardment before another assault was launched. It was the same as those further along the east of the line. Two closely-packed battalions advanced and met the same fate as every other German massed attack. They were cut down in droves as they emerged from a wood a mere 200 metres from the East Surreys' defensive line. The German soldiers continued to advance despite their severe losses, but courage alone was not sufficient. A British officer later remembered walking down the line, hitting his men on their backsides with his sword and telling them to fire low. The range was so short that many were firing high.

On the extreme left, the 1st Duke of Cornwall's Light Infantry did not get into action until 4.45pm, when they easily repulsed a horde of German cavalry. Shortly afterwards, the 7th and 8th Divisions of the German IV Corps found the left flank of the British position at the bridge at Pommeroeul and Condé. It was 5pm. Von Kluck had finally fumbled his way to a decisive point but it was too late. The British beat back the mass assaults as they had elsewhere. The defenders were hardly troubled, and repulsed the initial German attacks easily. If IV Corps' onslaught had been co-ordinated with those of III and IX Corps, von Kluck could have struck a decisive blow. As it was, the piecemeal blows at the British position had achieved little of value.

Elsewhere, the outnumbered BEF was coming under increasing pressure. It was only a matter of time before the enemy would be across the canal in force. Even so, nine-and-a-half British battalions had held four German divisions at bay for much of the day.

BELOW **British troops, probably from the 1st Northumberland Fusiliers of 9 Brigade, at Jemappes, 22 August 1914. The local population turned out to greet them and feed them. (Mons Museum)**

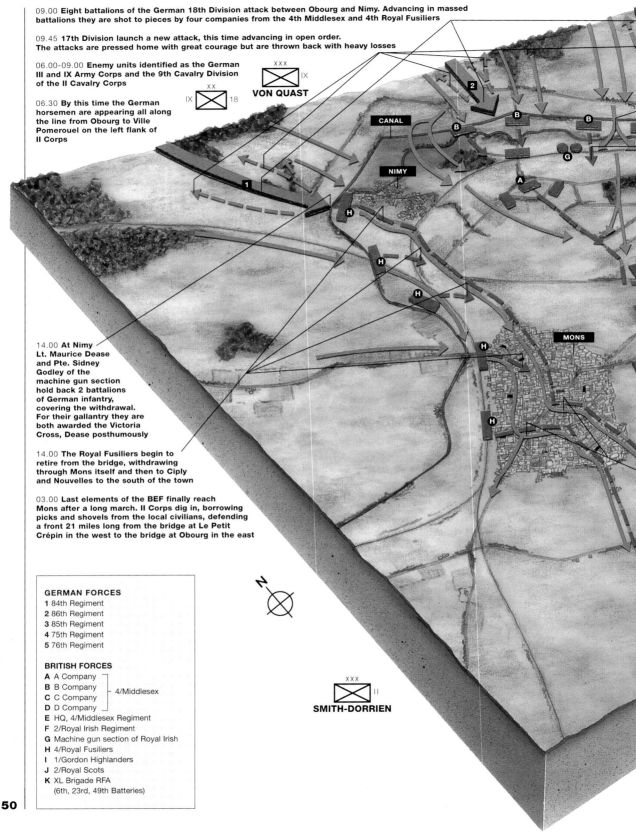

09.00 Eight battalions of the German 18th Division attack between Obourg and Nimy. Advancing in massed battalions they are shot to pieces by four companies from the 4th Middlesex and 4th Royal Fusiliers

09.45 17th Division launch a new attack, this time advancing in open order. The attacks are pressed home with great courage but are thrown back with heavy losses

06.00-09.00 Enemy units identified as the German III and IX Army Corps and the 9th Cavalry Division of the II Cavalry Corps

06.30 By this time the German horsemen are appearing all along the line from Obourg to Ville Pomerouel on the left flank of II Corps

XXX
IX

VON QUAST

XX
IX   18

CANAL

NIMY

2

B

B

B

G

A

MONS

14.00 At Nimy Lt. Maurice Dease and Pte. Sidney Godley of the machine gun section hold back 2 battalions of German infantry, covering the withdrawal. For their gallantry they are both awarded the Victoria Cross, Dease posthumously

14.00 The Royal Fusiliers begin to retire from the bridge, withdrawing through Mons itself and then to Ciply and Nouvelles to the south of the town

03.00 Last elements of the BEF finally reach Mons after a long march. II Corps dig in, borrowing picks and shovels from the local civilians, defending a front 21 miles long from the bridge at Le Petit Crépin in the west to the bridge at Obourg in the east

H

H

H

H

H

N

GERMAN FORCES
1 84th Regiment
2 86th Regiment
3 85th Regiment
4 75th Regiment
5 76th Regiment

BRITISH FORCES
A A Company
B B Company
C C Company   } 4/Middlesex
D D Company
E HQ, 4/Middlesex Regiment
F 2/Royal Irish Regiment
G Machine gun section of Royal Irish
H 4/Royal Fusiliers
I 1/Gordon Highlanders
J 2/Royal Scots
K XL Brigade RFA
     (6th, 23rd, 49th Batteries)

XXX
II

SMITH-DORRIEN

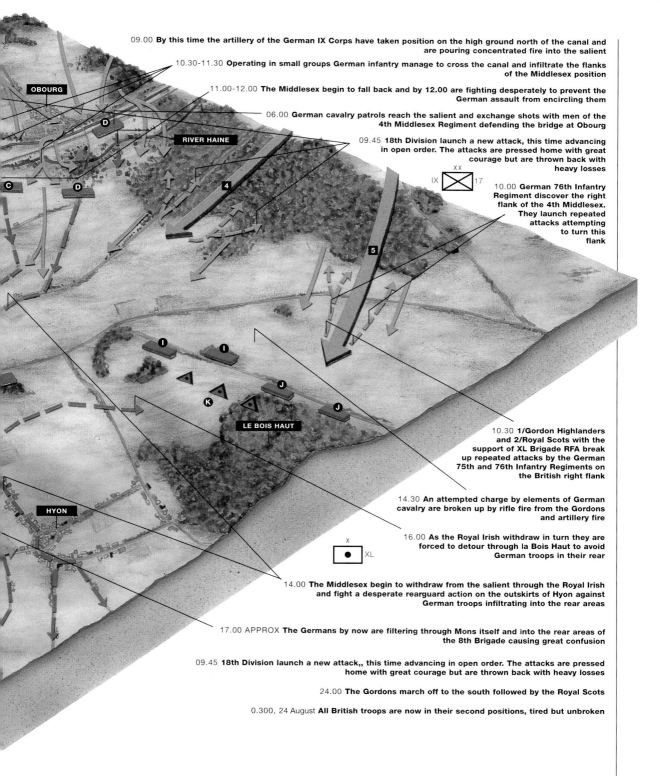

09.00 By this time the artillery of the German IX Corps have taken position on the high ground north of the canal and are pouring concentrated fire into the salient

10.30-11.30 Operating in small groups German infantry manage to cross the canal and infiltrate the flanks of the Middlesex position

11.00-12.00 The Middlesex begin to fall back and by 12.00 are fighting desperately to prevent the German assault from encircling them

06.00 German cavalry patrols reach the salient and exchange shots with men of the 4th Middlesex Regiment defending the bridge at Obourg

09.45 18th Division launch a new attack, this time advancing in open order. The attacks are pressed home with great courage but are thrown back with heavy losses

10.00 German 76th Infantry Regiment discover the right flank of the 4th Middlesex. They launch repeated attacks attempting to turn this flank

OBOURG

RIVER HAINE

LE BOIS HAUT

HYON

10.30 1/Gordon Highlanders and 2/Royal Scots with the support of XL Brigade RFA break up repeated attacks by the German 75th and 76th Infantry Regiments on the British right flank

14.30 An attempted charge by elements of German cavalry are broken up by rifle fire from the Gordons and artillery fire

16.00 As the Royal Irish withdraw in turn they are forced to detour through la Bois Haut to avoid German troops in their rear

14.00 The Middlesex begin to withdraw from the salient through the Royal Irish and fight a desperate rearguard action on the outskirts of Hyon against German troops infiltrating into the rear areas

17.00 APPROX The Germans by now are filtering through Mons itself and into the rear areas of the 8th Brigade causing great confusion

09.45 18th Division launch a new attack,, this time advancing in open order. The attacks are pressed home with great courage but are thrown back with heavy losses

24.00 The Gordons march off to the south followed by the Royal Scots

0.300, 24 August All British troops are now in their second positions, tired but unbroken

DEFENCE OF THE SALIENT

23 August 1914, 06.00-19.00 approx., viewed from the south-west showing the German attacks against the bridges, attempts to turn the British right flank and the British withdrawal

LEFT **A barrier of carts and wagons being constructed across the road from Mons to Quesney on 23 August 1914. Again, the local inhabitants willingly assisted the British troops. (Mons Museum)**

BELOW **A house in Mons being barricaded during the evening of 22 August 1914. These troops may well be from the 1st Battalion, Royal Scots Fusiliers. There are a number of soldiers on the upper storeys of the house and even after more than eighty years something of the picnic atmosphere that pervaded the BEF comes through. (Mons Museum)**

Just before the battle: Two private soldiers of the 1st Gordon Highlanders and two medical orderlies of the 2nd Royal Irish, troops of the 8th Infantry Brigade, pictured on the Mons-Beaumont main road on the morning of Sunday, 23 August 1914. Civilian onlookers mingle happily with the soldiers. Shortly after this photograph was taken, the area came under attack by the 17th Division. (Mons Museum)

Blowing the bridges

The slow withdrawal from the salient was repeated along the line of the canal, not as a general retreat or retirement, but in a series of independent movements. Platoons and companies pulled back as their positions became impossible to hold. The Northumberland Fusiliers stayed on the canal line to cover the efforts of Capt. Theodore Wright of the Royal Engineers to destroy the Mariette road bridge. Despite repeated attempts, and suffering from two bad wounds, he did not succeed, but received the Victoria Cross for his gallantry under the most persistent German fire. At Jemappes, L/Cpl. Charles Jarvis also won a Victoria Cross. In spite of heavy German fire, he worked alone for 90 minutes to bring down the bridge covered by the 1st Royal Scots.

The sound of the bridges being blown was the signal for the British infantry to make its way back to the shorter defensive line that Smith-Dorrien had already earmarked. Not all of the bridges were destroyed; a shortage of exploders left some intact. The Germans failed to capitalise on this. The rough handling they had received at the hands of the BEF had left them understandably hesitant about rushing forward.

The final attack of the day was launched against the 1st Gordons and 2nd Royal Scots who were still holding the eastern slope of Bois la Haut along the line of the road from Harmignies to Mons. German troops had already advanced through Mons and reached the rear of the British position. They ambushed the 23rd Battery of the Royal Artillery as it descended from the summit. The leading teams and drivers went down, but the Gordons promptly counterattacked just as a further assault developed on their front. It was a critical period, but the Gordons and the Royal Scots, supported by two companies of the Royal Irish Rifles, were well entrenched. Their devastating musketry annihilated the assault. The 75th (7th Bremen) Regiment der Infanterie alone lost five

BLOWING THE BRIDGE AT JEMAPPES, 23 AUGUST 1914

As the retreat continued along the line to the west of Mons the destruction of the bridges over the canal would have been a great achievement. Lance Corporal Charles Jarvis set the charges under Nimy bridge, pausing only to send his assistants from the Royal Scots Fusiliers back to their company as the fire became too intense. Having worked for 90 minutes under fire and placing and setting 22 charges, Jarvis successfully demolished the bridge. He was awarded the Victoria Cross.

officers and 376 men in a matter of minutes. The German commanders had had enough. The British heard enemy bugles sound 'Cease Fire' all along the line. Unmolested, the 23rd Battery, joined by the 6th Battery, cleared its guns from the slopes and the Gordons and Royal Scots followed them.

This costly thrust, pressed home with enormous bravery, was the last of its type. There would be a significant change in German tactics. In the future, the field-grey infantry would use their full artillery support. This time the BEF were able to escape to their new defence line without further interference.

II Corps was pleased with itself. The canal bridges had been held until dusk and its soldiers knew that they had inflicted considerable damage on the enemy. They believed that, man for man, they were superior to their foe. 'It was like a Third Division team playing the First Division,' one soldier wrote home later, 'the Germans were beaten thorough.'

The total British loss during the day's fighting was 1,642 killed, wounded and missing. Of these, 40 came from Haig's I Corps on the right and south of Smith-Dorrien's line. II Corps had taken the brunt of the casualties and most of these were in the 4th Middlesex and the 1st Royal Irish Regiment. The Middlesex lost more than 400 men, the Royal Irish over 300. German losses are more difficult to compute; their system of returns does not allow casualties for a particular action, or even day, to be easily established. Most estimates agree that they were not less than 6,000 and could have been as high as 10,000. Individual German soldiers fought with great gallantry and tenacity, but were defeated by the murderous fire of the British infantry.

THE RETREAT BEGINS

During the evening of 23 August, Sir John French finally accepted that the BEF was facing an enemy with an overwhelming superiority in numbers, and that Lanrezac's Fifth Army was withdrawing. The conclusion was inescapable. If the BEF did not retreat, its flanks would be left unprotected and it would be swallowed as von Kluck's First Army continued its relentless advance. Sir John's belief that he was being left in the lurch by his ally now became a major feature of his thinking.

Instead of immediately issuing orders to his corps commanders, Sir John French sent for their chief staff officers. He announced his intention to pull back the BEF eight miles and instructed the corps commanders to work out the order of retirement among themselves. The only definite instruction was that I Corps would cover II Corps by occupying a line from Feignies to Bavai. Because of this peculiar and time-consuming procedure, Smith-Dorrien did not receive the order

To German minds, the tiny BEF represented no threat at all. It was the French who were the major enemy and it was deeds of gallantry and crushing victories against the despised French which filled contemporary German newspapers and magazines. Postcards also glorified the defeat of a traditional enemy – this one shows Uhlans capturing French artillery pieces with remarkable ease. (Michael Solka)

until 3am in the morning of 24 August. His headquarters was, in any event, without a working telegraph or telephone line and it was not until 4.30am that the first of his battalions was told to withdraw.

Von Kluck now had some idea of the location and strength of the BEF and decided to force it back to the fortress of Maubeuge where it could be bottled up. He reasoned also that the British would try to retire towards the Channel ports, so he sent II Cavalry Corps under von Marwitz to head them off and decided to envelop the British left in order to stifle any attempt by the BEF to retreat west. Accordingly, he had made little attempt to attack I Corps on the right; it was the left flank that would need to feel the pressure. II Corps would again find itself outnumbered and fighting desperately against a determined and gallant foe.

Sir John French had already considered and resisted the temptation to retire behind the walls of Maubeuge. He was only too aware of the fate of Marshal Bazaine at Metz in 1870 who had 'in clinging to Metz, acted like one who, when the ship is foundering, should lay hold of the anchor'. The BEF was instructed to fall back towards Le Cateau.

Von Kluck's attacks on 24 August were a catalogue of errors and mis-understandings. Haig received the orders to retire before Smith-Dorrien. At 4am, 1st Division of I Corps began to move out, followed some 45 minutes later by the 2nd Division. The German IX Corps received no orders to chase I Corps until 8am, by which time Haig had moved his men too far away to be engaged with any realistic chance of being driven into Maubeuge. Despatching von Marwitz's cavalry to the west had been von Kluck's first serious mistake in his attempts to destroy the BEF. This was his second.

II Corps runs into trouble

Smith-Dorrien already had two major problems before he could extricate his troops. His first was to clear unit transport from the roads, which had been brought up to support the general advance and was the reason why the BEF had marched to Mons in the first place. This was not

LEFT **To the right of the 4th Royal Fusiliers, the 4th Middlesex and the 2nd Royal Irish Regiment spent 23 August 1914 in a ferocious defence of their position against odds calculated of at least six to one. They faced elements of both the 17th and 18th Divisions as well as the artillery of IX Corps. XL Brigade of the RFA with their 18-pounders caused great havoc amongst the attackers. (Mons Museum)**

BELOW **When the 4th Middlesex finally retired, they left behind one of their drums which was subsequently retrieved from the battlefield and hidden from the Germans. At the end of the war, the drum and three from other units recovered after the battle, were proudly displayed in the Mons Museum. In the inter-war years, they were joined by a further 22 drums presented by regiments who had fought in the battle. The 4th Middlesex drum still hangs, with its companions, in a place of honour in the Museum. (Author's Collection)**

a simple task and was made worse by the hordes of refugees already on the limited number of roads. The second problem was a manoeuvre which was complicated under peacetime conditions let alone when in imminent danger of enemy assault. Smith-Dorrien had decided to switch the positions of his two divisions. The 3rd, which had taken the brunt of the German attacks the previous day, would retire first. The 5th Division would follow and have less distance to cover when it began its withdrawal on the left.

If Smith-Dorrien had received his orders earlier, he could probably have withdrawn in the darkness unmolested. As it was, a severe German bombardment started before dawn, initially against the British positions in the villages of Ciply and Frameries, but rapidly extending along the whole of 3 Division's front as far as Wasmes and Hornu. The lessons of the previous day had not been lost on the German commanders. To the assault infantry, waiting impatiently for the barrage to lift, it seemed as if the British would be easy targets. Ciply and Frameries were occupied by the 2nd South Lancashires and the 1st Lincolns. They were the rearguards of the 7th and 9th Brigades and were supported by 109 Battery of the Royal Field Artillery.

The repulse of the German 6th Division

The barrage ceased and the British troops gazed yet again on the now familiar sight of a mass infantry attack. The two battalions were about to feel the full weight of an assault by the entire 6th Division of III Corps. Ordered to hold British attention in the centre while the attack on the British left flank was being prepared, units of the 24th Brandenburg Regiment, the 20th Infantry Regiment and the 64th Infantry Regiment,

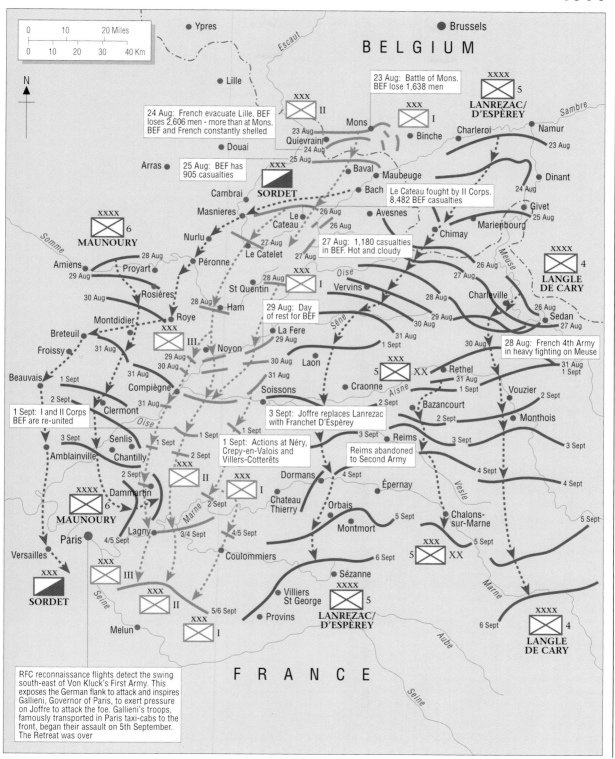

BELGIUM

Ypres ● ● Brussels

0 — 10 — 20 Miles
0 — 10 — 20 — 30 — 40 Km

N

Lille ●

23 Aug: Battle of Mons. BEF lose 1,638 men

XXXX 5
LANREZAC/ D'ESPÈREY

24 Aug: French evacuate Lille. BEF loses 2,606 men - more than at Mons. BEF and French constantly shelled

XXX II

XXX I

Mons
Quievrain
23 Aug
24 Aug
25 Aug

Binche

Charleroi

Namur ●
Sambre
23 Aug

● Douai

Baval

Maubeuge

Dinant ●

Arras ●

25 Aug: BEF has 905 casualties

XXX
SORDET

Bach

Le Cateau fought by II Corps. 8,482 BEF casualties

24 Aug

25 Aug

Givet ●

Cambrai
Masnieres

Le Cateau
26 Aug

Avesnes

Marienbourg

26 Aug

XXXX 6
MAUNOURY

Nurlu
Le Catelet

27 Aug: 1,180 casualties in BEF. Hot and cloudy

Chimay

Meuse

XXXX 4
LANGLE DE CARY

Somme

28 Aug

Péronne
27 Aug

Oise

26 Aug

27 Aug

Charleville

Amiens
29 Aug

Proyart

St Quentin
28 Aug

XXX I

Vervins

28 Aug

Sedan
26 Aug
27 Aug

30 Aug

Rosiéres

Ham
28 Aug

29 Aug: Day of rest for BEF

Sène

30 Aug

29 Aug

Montdidier

Roye

XXX III

Noyon

Laon

31 Aug
1 Sept

28 Aug: French 4th Army in heavy fighting on Meuse

Breteuil

29 Aug
30 Aug

La Fere
29 Aug

30 Aug

XXX XX 5

Rethel
31 Aug

31 Aug
1 Sept

Froissy

31 Aug

Compiègne
31 Aug

30 Aug

Soissons
31 Aug

Craonne

Aisne

1 Sept

Vouzier
2 Sept

Beauvais
1 Sept

Oise

2 Sept

3 Sept: Joffre replaces Lanrezac with Franchet D'Espèrey

2 Sept

Bazancourt
2 Sept

Monthois

2 Sept

Clermont
31 Aug

1 Sept: I and II Corps BEF are re-united

3 Sept

Senlis

1 Sept

2 Sept

1 Sept: Actions at Néry, Crepy-en-Valois and Villers-Cotterêts

Reims
3 Sept

3 Sept

Amblainville

Chantilly

XXX II

XXX I

Dormans

Reims abandoned to Second Army

Épernay

Vesle

4 Sept

4 Sept

XXXX 6
MAUNOURY

Dammartin

2 Sept

Chateau Thierry

Orbais

4 Sept

Chalons-sur-Marne

5 Sept

Paris ●

Lagny
4/5 Sept

3/4 Sept

4/5 Sept

Montmort

5 Sept

XXX XX 5

5 Sept

Versailles ●

XXX III

Coulommiers

6 Sept

Marne

6 Sept

XXX
SORDET

Seine

XXX III

XXX II
5/6 Sept

Villiers St George

Sézanne ●

XXXX 5
LANREZAC/ D'ESPÈREY

Aube

Melun ●

XXX I

Provins ●

6 Sept

XXXX 4
LANGLE DE CARY

F R A N C E

Seine

RFC reconnaissance flights detect the swing south-east of Von Kluck's First Army. This exposes the German flank to attack and inspires Gallieni, Governor of Paris, to exert pressure on Joffre to attack the foe. Gallieni's troops, famously transported in Paris taxi-cabs to the front, began their assault on 5th September. The Retreat was over among others, surged forward, fully confident that the British would have been totally cowed by the artillery fire.

It was the German infantry who suffered. The bombardment had been peculiarly ineffective in the built-up area. There had been much noise, dust and falling masonry which served merely to provide extra cover for the defenders. As the Germans advanced, they once again ran into the devastating rifle fire of the regular British soldier. 'Tommy seems to have waited,' wrote one German officer later, 'for the moment of the assault. He had carefully studied our training manuals, and suddenly, when we were well in the open, he turned his machine guns on.' The greatest tribute to the musketry of the BEF was the consistent German belief that they faced massed machine guns.

To add to the attackers' woes, 109 Battery opened up with shrapnel as the German troops went forward. The advance was shredded, casualties in the assaulting units running at 30 to 40 per cent. Gallantry was not enough. The Germans broke under a hail of rifle fire and shrapnel and fell back to their start line.

In the lull that followed, the 8th Brigade, made up of the sorely tried 4th Middlesex, 1st Gordon Highlanders, 2nd Royal Scots and 2nd Royal Irish Regiment was able to get away from Nouvelles without difficulty.

A new artillery bombardment followed, and a new mass assault. The result was the same. If anything, German losses were even heavier this time. The 1st Lincolns and 2nd South Lancashires kept firing, the enemy soldiers kept falling. The attack was beaten off, and at 9am the 9th Brigade withdrew from Frameries in good order, the rearguard of 1st Lincolns keeping a tight watch on advance parties of German infantry.

Finally, and after some delay, it was time for 7th Brigade to pull out of the neighbouring village of Ciply. Their route led through Frameries and the retreat of the rearguard through the village proved to be costly. There had been enough time for the Germans to set up machine guns in enfilade among the slag heaps. Originally intending to fire upon the 1st Lincolns, the German gunners wreaked severe damage upon the 2nd South Lancashires as they pulled back. Nearly 300 men were lost in a very short time, more than half of 3 Division's total casualties that day.

German losses in the attacks on Frameries and Ciply are not known. They were certainly very high. The 24th Brandenburg alone lost three out of six company commanders, half of its remaining officers and one third of its men. It is without question that the German infantry made no effort to pursue and, in the words of the Official History, 'handled 3rd Division on this day with singular respect'.

The 5th Division face von Kluck

To the left of the British line, the 5th Division was less fortunate. They had been largely untroubled during the battle of Mons, their total casualties being less than 400. They would now receive a proper baptism as von Kluck tried to turn the British flank. The 5th Division would be attacked by three German divisions that day – the 6th Division of III Corps and the whole of IV Corps.

The defensive line ran north-west from Paturages to Hornu. The 2nd Duke of Wellingtons held the Paturages position and Hornu was covered

The 4th Middlesex were ably supported by the 2nd Royal Irish during their action. Amongst the day's heroes was QMS T.W. Fitzpatrick of that regiment. Cut off from his unit, he defended the La Bascule cross-roads on the eastern outskirts of Mons from noon until sunset with 40 men who were mostly bandsmen. Seven were killed and 17 were so severely wounded that they were unable to move. At midnight, Fitzpatrick retired with the 16 others across the hills of Panisel and Bois-le-Haut to rejoin his battalion the next day near Quey-le-Grand. For his exploits he was awarded the Distinguished Conduct Medal. Later commissioned, he finished the war as a colonel. (Mons Museum)

The Band of the 2nd Royal Irish Regiment shortly before the war. It was these men who were led by QMS Fitzpatrick in his defence of the La Bascule crossroads. (Mons Museum)

by the 1st Bedfords and 1st Dorsets. The German artillery began its preparatory bombardment at about 8.30am. Once the artillery fire ceased at about 10am, the same familiar pattern was seen, as the German infantry, drawn from the 5th Division and part of 6th Division of III Corps, came forward in column to be met by rapid rifle fire and close-range shrapnel from the British artillery. The conflict developed rapidly into a confused series of running fire-fights among the slag-heaps and cottages. The individual training given to the British soldier again showed its worth as personal ingenuity and courage came into their own. 37th Battery of the Royal Field Artillery at Hornu fired its howitzers 'as if they were machine guns', while the infantry, in small groups, repeatedly drove back the German attacks.

The 12th Brandenburg Grenadiers, who had suffered so badly the day before on the canal when they met the Royal West Kents, had another testing time. They came under fire not only from the British, but from their own artillery as well. As a result, the regiment seems effectively to have been wiped out.

By about 11am, 5th Division began its retirement, pulling back as the 3rd Division on its right began its withdrawal. There were some incidents. The 20th Infantry Regiment, used in the attack on Frameries, was able to infiltrate the British position, but its ambush of the Dorsets' regimental transport was remarkably unsuccessful, lacking both energy and enterprise, and the transport escaped unscathed.

More costly was the failure to get withdrawal orders to the 2nd Duke of Wellingtons. Together with their artillery, and reinforced by two companies of the Royal West Kents, they held on to their original positions and came under heavy German artillery and small arms fire. Losses rose,

but when the Germans finally came forward en masse to deliver the final blow, they received a devastating hail of fire which stopped them in their tracks and allowed the defenders to slip away. Six German battalions had been held at a cost of nearly 400 casualties.

It was on the left flank that matters became really serious, with a situation developing during the morning which could have destroyed the whole of II Corps. The independent 19th Infantry Brigade and the Cavalry Division had retired without mishap earlier in the day. Apart from some desultory firing before first light, there had been few signs of the Germans – not surprisingly, because von Marwitz's cavalry had left to patrol the routes to the Channel ports. By 11.30am, at just the time when the 2nd Duke of Wellingtons was beating back their last attack, the

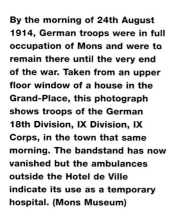

By the morning of 24th August 1914, German troops were in full occupation of Mons and were to remain there until the very end of the war. Taken from an upper floor window of a house in the Grand-Place, this photograph shows troops of the German 18th Division, IX Division, IX Corps, in the town that same morning. The bandstand has now vanished but the ambulances outside the Hotel de Ville indicate its use as a temporary hospital. (Mons Museum)

Par ordre du Commandant de la Place HAUPTMANN VON WARTENBERG :

Tous les Soldats Anglais pouvant marcher doivent se trouver à l'hôtel de ville, **AVEC LEURS ARMES AUJOURD'HUI AVANT SIX HEURES.**

S'il en existe qui sont blessés ou ne peuvent marcher, les habitants chez lesquels ils se trouvent, doivent en faire la **DÉCLARATION à L'HOTEL-DE-VILLE AVANT SIX HEURES du SOIR.**

Si ces ordres ne sont pas suivis, le Commandant de la Place peut frapper la Ville de Mons d'un impôt de guerre très considérable.

Mons, le 25 Août 1914.
Par ordre,
le Bourgmestre,
Jean LESCARTS.

Imprimerie et Lithographie THÉNARD-VLEMINCX, Rue de la Petite-Guirlande, 16, Mons.

Numbers of wounded British soldiers were rescued by the civilian inhabitants of Mons who hid them from the invader. Posters – this one dated 25 August 1914 – warned the population of dire retribution if they sheltered British soldiers. This one demands that all English soldiers capable of walking are to report to the town hall with their arms before 6pm. If soldiers were so badly hurt that they could not report in person, the citizen finding them was to make a declaration to that effect. Failure to do so would result in a considerable communal fine upon the town. Despite this threat – and worse – the local population helped many soldiers to evade capture and eventually rejoin their units. A few stayed hidden in the vicinity throughout the whole period of the war. (Mons Museum)

Cavalry Division and the 19th Brigade were back behind the left of the 5th Division.

At this point the full weight of IV Corps artillery opened up from the Quievrain area against the now exposed flank of the British line. Von Kluck had at last got the right hook into operation, and the whole of IV Corps, consisting of the German 7th and 8th Divisions, was taking part. Von Kluck's aim was to swing round against Elouges, smash against the flank of the 5th Division and send it reeling towards Maubeuge. The steady withdrawal of the 5th Division could have been turned into a rout.

The commander of the 5th Division, Maj.-Gen. Sir Charles Fergusson, sent for help to the Cavalry Division. Allenby responded swiftly, sending the 2nd and 3rd Cavalry Brigades, supported by 'D', 'E' and 'L' Batteries of the Royal Horse Artillery. In the interim, Fergusson despatched his last remaining reserves, the 1st Norfolks, 1st Cheshires and 119 Battery of the RHA, all under the command of Col. Ballard of the Norfolks, to face the four German divisions advancing towards the gap between Elouges and Audregnies about two miles away. The orders were simple: they must stop the German advance.

The Flank Guard action at Elouges

In the following action, two British infantry battalions, four batteries of artillery and parts of two cavalry brigades faced 24 battalions of German infantry and nine artillery batteries on a battlefield of some six square miles. If von Marwitz's cavalry had also been available to the Germans, then 5th Division would have been annihilated.

The British infantry had no time to dig in. The Cheshires took the left of the line, the Lincolns the right, with 119 Battery along a little ridge which gave them a clear field of fire across the cornfields towards Quievrain. The position was soon reinforced by the arrival of the 2nd Cavalry Brigade. The 9th Lancers and the 4th Dragoon Guards took up a position away on the left of the British line.

At 12.45pm, at least six battalions of German infantry, supported by six or more batteries of artillery, started their advance in two columns from Quievrain and Basieux. Their route led them across the front of the British cavalry and the target they presented was too much for the cavalry to resist. An order to attack the enemy infantry, if necessary by mounted action, became the signal for an all-out charge.

The 9th Lancers, with two troops of the 4th Dragoons, immediately galloped towards the enemy who were about 2,000 yards away. They came under fire as the German infantry reacted and the charge was brought to an ignominious halt by a wire fence bordering a sugar factory. As men and horses milled about, they were an easy target for the German guns. Most of the cavalry went to the right, some taking cover behind the sugar factory and some slag heaps, the others galloping across the front of the British infantry before re-forming. The gesture – one which Wellington would certainly have recognised and abhorred – cost 250 men and 300 horses and had little effect on the German advance which continued with hardly a pause.

Nonetheless, the action, much magnified and distorted by the popular press, became an important ingredient in boosting morale in Britain. It became known as the 'Charge to Save the Guns', harking back to earlier wars in which wire fences and machine guns were unknown.

63

A rare photograph of wounded British survivors of the battle with their Belgian rescuers. Taken only a few days after the flight, the location is the Hornu-Wasmes mine. The colliery sick bay was used as an operating theatre and hospital and some 40 British officers and men were hidden there. The Germans did not discover the British wounded until early September by which time some had already made an escape. Others got away subsequently, being passed down escape routes which included, amongst others, that operated by Nurse Edith Cavell. (Mons Museum)

Mons remained under German occupation until the end of the war and the museum provides a valuable record of the period. There are sections devoted to the French, Belgian and Italian armies as well as the German invaders. (Author's Collection)

A mile further to the west, the 3rd Cavalry Brigade was north of Angre. Supported by the 13-pdrs. of 'D' and 'E' Batteries of the RHA, they also charged the right flank of the German 8th Division, the 4th Hussars leading, supported by the 5th Lancers. Their losses were not as heavy but, again, they only marginally delayed the German onslaught.

The six guns of 'L' Battery, positioned to the left of the Cheshires, came into action at 1pm and began to sweep the advancing Germans with enfilading fire. At 2,000 yards range, the shrapnel tore great holes in the masses of enemy infantry. Hardly surprisingly, the German infantry stopped short and retreated. Re-formed, they tried again, displaying remarkable bravery, but with the same shattering results. All along the line, the pattern was repeated. By all military logic, the British troops should have been quickly steam-rolled into oblivion, but they continued to fight against odds which were at least six to one.

Checked on the left, the Germans tried to work themselves further south, outside the range of the defenders. On the right of the British line, the assault from the 7th Division began to press more heavily. German tactics were altering in response to the stubborn defence; counter battery fire against the RHA was largely inaccurate, but was causing problems. 'L' Battery itself was attacked by four German batteries, but suffered only 12 casualties. On the right, 119 Battery fared rather worse. It lost 30 men, one-quarter of its strength, and came under fire from three German batteries as well as machine guns at close range.

By mid-afternoon it was clear that the position could not be held; the rest of 5th Division had retired safely and it was time for the rearguard to disengage. 119 Battery withdrew under intense fire, its guns being manhandled away by the gunners and a group of 9th Lancers. Two Victoria Crosses were won at this stage, one going to the battery commander, Maj. Alexander, the other to Capt. Francis Grenfell of the 9th Lancers.

Remarkably, the artillery did not lose a single gun in the engagement, even though every battery left under enemy fire. In the three hours in which they were in action, each battery fired about 450 rounds and caused havoc among the enemy troops.

By 5pm, with the artillery safely to the rear and the cavalry falling back, Col. Ballard ordered the infantry to retire. The Norfolks managed to withdraw but the message, sent three times, never reached the Cheshires. They continued to hold their line, stubbornly resisting for a further three hours, and causing heavy casualties among the German infantry. As the German attacks continued, the battalion was slowly split into small groups some of which were finally overwhelmed by ever-increasing numbers. Others managed to slip away, but the action cost the Cheshires some 800 casualties, killed, wounded and missing.

II Corps, led by an exceptional soldier, Horace Smith-Dorrien, had once again completely frustrated the enemy's attacks. The British casualties for the day were more than 2,000, of which 1,650 were in the 5th Division. I Corps had again escaped most of the fighting, its losses amounting to about 100 men. On the German side, the attack on the rearguard alone is estimated to have cost some 3,000 to 5,000 men; combined with the costly efforts on the right of the British line, the total loss has been estimated at anything between 6,000 and 10,000 casualties. The disappearance of some regiments from the order of battle suggests that it may have been far worse.

There were tangible results to the day's fighting although they were not immediately apparent. Von Kluck's advance had been slowed. During the whole day, his army had covered just over three miles and the BEF had eluded his grasp yet again. Despite an overall superiority in men and in guns, he had failed to destroy the BEF. It was an error for which the German Army would pay a high price.

Hungry, exhausted, the British troops stumbled into their rest areas. New orders had already arrived from GHQ: 'The Army will move tomorrow, 25th inst,' began Operation Order No 7, 'to a position in the neighbourhood of Le Cateau, exact positions will be pointed out on the ground tomorrow.' The Retreat continued.

Many photographs purporting to show British troops on the Retreat from Mons were, in fact, taken at the time of the Battle of Loos by Paul Maze, a French liaison officer. This, however, is the genuine article. An RFA crew, with 18-pounder gun and limber, shortly after being in action – note the empty shell cases.

This helpful Boy Scout, with the British cavalry, is carrying a Lee-Enfield rifle and wearing an ammunition bandolier as well as other British Army-issue items – one of which appears to be an infantry webbing belt. This suggests a date during the retreat itself. The town is clearly in a French-speaking area and the tramlines suggest a substantial community. Boy Scouts were not generally employed as combatants but, equipped as above, this one would incur the considerable wrath of any German soldier who met him and would hardly escape a firing squad. (Private Collection)

Retreat to Le Cateau

By the morning of 25 August, Sir John French thought only of saving the BEF in accordance, as he believed, with Kitchener's instructions. Co-operation with the French was forgotten. The British Commander-in-Chief entertained some astounding ideas. One plan was to retreat pell-mell to Le Havre, turning the port into a fort, until the BEF was ready to fight again. That this manoeuvre would have required a march across the whole front of von Kluck's advancing troops is sufficient comment on its practicability.

There was one piece of good news. Kitchener had sent the 4th Division as reinforcements. It arrived in the battle area on the 24th, minus its cavalry, cyclists, signallers, field ambulances, engineers, ammunition columns and heavy artillery. Nevertheless, it was a welcome and valuable addition to the steadily diminishing numbers of the BEF.

Retreat to Le Cateau produced a problem. To the rear of I and II Corps was the Mormal Forest, roughly ten miles long and four miles wide. Two roads ran from east to west across the wood, only a few rough tracks ran from north to south, the direction in which the BEF was travelling. The dangers in trying to squeeze along them were obvious. The only choice was to use the roads on either side of the wood. To move the whole of the BEF down one side or the other would cause even more chaos and confusion on the crowded roads, create delays and possibly expose the BEF to another onslaught from the German First Army.

Sir John French decided, with some misgivings, to split the BEF in two; I Corps would retreat down the eastern side of the wood, II Corps would withdraw down the west and the BEF would be reunited at Le Cateau, 25 miles to the south.

Additionally, there were supply problems. Everything had been planned in the expectation that the BEF would be advancing northwards, not retreating southwards. The forward dumps had been overrun and the lines of communication disrupted. With limited telephone facilities and constant movement, it became impossible to discover where individual units were and what they needed. In a brilliant piece of improvisation, Maj.-Gen. Robertson, the BEF's Quartermaster-General, ordered his men to off-load supplies at every crossroads and junction along the line of the retreat.

Both Haig and Smith-Dorrien faced difficulties. I Corps was faced with a meandering route which first crossed the River Sambre and then re-crossed it on two later occasions. The problems were exacerbated because the road was crammed with soldiers from Lanrezac's Fifth Army as well as hordes of refugees. In the stifling August heat, I Corps averaged only about two miles per hour as it trudged wearily onwards. To add to Haig's woes, he was suffering severely from diarrhoea, a condition which hardly helped his concentration or normally imperturbable reactions.

Fortunately, there was little sign of the foe. The BEF was eight miles south of Von Kluck when it halted the previous evening. The First Army commander was still essentially mistaken about the movements of the BEF and believed he had succeeded in pushing it towards Maubeuge. Further, he assumed that he had forced the whole of the BEF, six divisions as he believed, in that direction. The location of Haig's I Corps was unknown to him. Reacting to a series of confusing and contradictory reports, von Kluck gave orders for the First Army to wheel south-east. It was a movement which in fact took them behind the rear of II Corps and towards the flank of I Corps.

Landrecies

Apart from odd skirmishes with advanced patrols, I Corps spent another day out of reach of the enemy. As evening approached, the tired troops began to reach their billets. The Corps HQ went to Landrecies, where there was a bridge over the Sambre, sharing the village with the 4th (Guards) Brigade. The 6th Brigade settled down further east at Maroilles, two miles from another crossing point of the Sambre.

For the advance elements of the German III and IV Corps, it was also a tiring day. They, too, were looking forward to settling down in billets for the night. The 14th Regiment der Infanterie of III Corps was anticipating a quiet time at Landrecies; the 48th Regiment der Infanterie was equally anxious to reach Maroilles.

Shortly after Haig reached Landrecies at about 4pm, a flood of refugees arrived and claimed that German Uhlans were close behind them. A check revealed no sign of the enemy, but prudently, No 3 Company of the 3rd Battalion Coldstream Guards, with two machine-guns, went to the north-west to guard the road from Le Quesnoy. The remainder of the brigade prepared defences in the town itself.

At Maroilles, two troops of the 15th Hussars were guarding the bridge when the first patrols of the 48th Infantry arrived. There was a fierce skirmish which lasted nearly an hour before the Germans brought up a field gun. The Hussars fell back and were then reinforced by the 1st Royal Berkshires. It was 7pm and getting dark. In a sharp action

The stand by Smith-Dorrien's II Corps at Le Cateau is one of the great actions of the British Army. It was Allenby, admitting that his cavalry was 'pretty well played-out' whilst reporting that von Kluck's infantry were only a few hours distant, that decided Smith-Dorrien. Allenby proved to be an exceptional cavalry commander although he and his small staff suffered along with everyone else during the retreat. Most of their personal kit was lost and they could muster only one razor between them for several days! (Author's Collection)

involving savage hand-to-hand fighting along a stone causeway leading to the bridge, the Berkshires lost about 60 men. The Germans held on to the bridge and the frustrated Berkshires finally abandoned their attempts to take it.

It was dark at Landrecies when Capt. Monck, in command of the guard on the road, heard the sound of approaching troops. A challenge got a reply in French. A moment later the Coldstream were charged by the Germans. In the confusion, the Germans managed to snatch a machine gun but it was promptly recaptured.

No 1 Company of the Coldstream Guards came up as reinforcements. The German attacks continued, but each charge was thrown back by the steady fire of the Guards. By careful use of cover, the Germans eventually enfiladed the Coldstream line, forcing the Guards back towards a line of cottages. A small haystack was set on fire and by its light a single German field gun was able to shell the British position at close range. Pte. West of the Coldstream Guards twice dashed out under heavy fire and managed to put out the flames.

The fighting went on until after midnight, ending finally when a howitzer of 60 Battery arrived and disabled its German counterpart with its third round. A diversion was mounted by the Irish Guards and, eventually the disgruntled Germans withdrew to the southern edge of the Mormal Forest. Casualties on both sides were very similar. Twelve Coldstream Guardsmen had been killed, 105 were wounded and there were seven missing. The German official figures admitted 127 casualties, but with a higher proportion of killed. To the west of the town, the 2nd Battalion Grenadier Guards were involved in a series of confused actions. When the dawn came, their total losses amounted to seven men.

The affair at Landrecies was no more than a skirmish, but it was to have a profound effect. In the town itself, the belief rapidly spread that it was surrounded. Haig, normally calm and placid, reacted strongly to the reports he received. After giving orders for the defence of the town, he instructed his staff to burn all secret papers and resolved to sell his life dearly. After the first excitement had subsided, he reasoned that the enemy line was probably thin and decided that the Corps staff should make a bid to escape. This was sensible. Little would be gained if the whole of the Corps staff were taken prisoner.

Haig, with a combination of luck and judgement, was able to rejoin the main body of I Corps with his staff at about 1.30am. He immediately set about rescuing the 4th (Guards) Brigade from what he believed to be a difficult situation. The 1st Division was ordered to mount a rescue operation at dawn. He then telephoned GHQ to report the attack and he assessed the situation as 'very critical'. Two hours later, at 3.50am, he spoke again to GHQ, asking this time for Smith-Dorrien's II Corps, eight miles away on the other side of the Sambre, to be sent to help him. Haig believed that I Corps was about to be attacked in force.

Smith-Dorrien was unable to help. He had already decided that his only course of action was to stand and fight at Le Cateau, which was precisely where von Kluck's army was marching.

The progress of II Corps along the western side of the Mormal Forest was extremely difficult. The 3rd Division on the left of the Corps were harassed by von Kluck's right wing, which pushed forward in yet another attempt to outflank the weary BEF. Throughout the day, the rearguards of the 3rd Division, the 19th Infantry Brigade and the Cavalry Division fought a series of running engagements against an unenthusiastic enemy. Von Kluck's divisions were also suffering from the punishing marches along the sun-baked roads.

There was a sharp action at Le Quesnoy during the day when the 1st and 3rd Cavalry Brigades engaged in a fierce skirmish. At Solesmes, a small town on the route, there was considerable confusion as streams of refugees, transports and troops eddied around the narrow streets. A determined German attack at this point would have been disastrous; as it was, the 2nd South Lancashires and 1st Wiltshires, the rearguard of 7th Infantry Brigade, were able to discourage the tentative German IV Corps from approaching too closely. By mid-afternoon, the 3rd Division had disengaged, covered by two brigades of the 4th Division, leaving the Germans to settle down in and around Solesmes. The day's work had cost the cavalry more than 100 casualties, the infantry a further 350.

The 5th Division did not see the enemy at all, but their route to Le Cateau was thronged with civilian refugees, French soldiers and wagons of all types. Worst of all was the sweltering heat, and many men dropped out of the ranks. As evening came, there was a heavy thunderstorm. The troops who straggled into Le Cateau were wet, weary and very hungry.

Some of the British infantry positions at Le Cateau were far from ideal. This photograph purports to show part of the battle but is, without doubt, not the genuine article, either being posed or a film still. It nonetheless gives an idea of the actual fighting. (Private Collection)

The decision to fight

That evening GHQ ordered a continuation of the retreat south-westwards towards Peronne. Smith-Dorrien well knew the exhausted condition of his men and had grave doubts about how much more marching they could take; he had no information as to the location of Allenby's Cavalry or Gen. Snow's newly arrived 4th Division. He knew nothing of the rearguard action of the 3rd Division. None of them would be accounted for

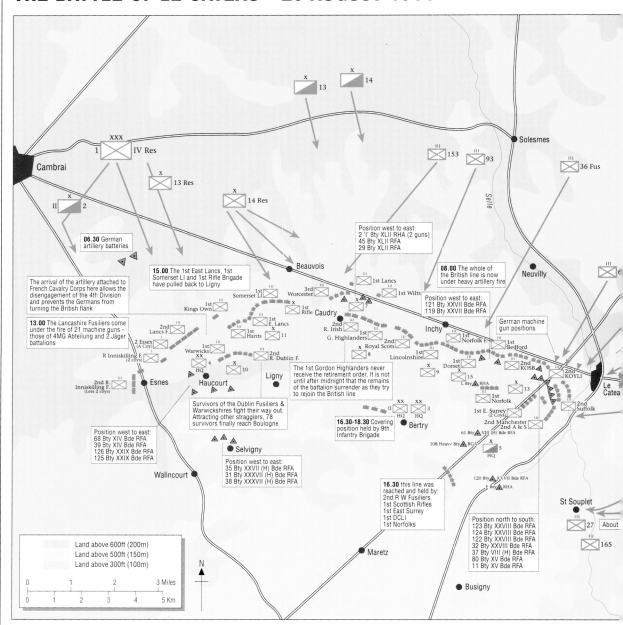

06.30 German artillery batteries

The arrival of the artillery attached to French Cavalry Corps here allows the disengagement of the 4th Division and prevents the Germans from turning the British flank

13.00 The Lancashire Fusiliers come under the fire of 21 machine guns - those of 4MG Abteilung and 2 Jäger battalions

15.00 The 1st East Lancs, 1st Somerset LI and 1st Rifle Brigade have pulled back to Ligny

Position west to east:
2 'I' Bty XLII RHA (2 guns)
45 Bty XLII RFA
29 Bty XLII RFA

08.00 The whole of the British line is now under heavy artillery fire

Position west to east:
121 Bty XXVII Bde RFA
119 Bty XXVII Bde RFA

German machine gun positions

The 1st Gordon Highlanders never receive the retirement order. It is not until after midnight that the remains of the battalion surrender as they try to rejoin the British line

Survivors of the Dublin Fusiliers & Warwickshires fight their way out. Attracting other stragglers, 78 survivors finally reach Boulogne

16.30-18.30 Covering position held by 9th Infantry Brigade

Position west to east:
68 Bty XIV Bde RFA
39 Bty XIV Bde RFA
126 Bty XXIX Bde RFA
125 Bty XXIX Bde RFA

Position west to east:
35 Bty XXVII (H) Bde RFA
31 Bty XXXVII (H) Bde RFA
38 Bty XXXVII (H) Bde RFA

16.30 this line was reached and held by:
2nd R W Fusiliers
1st Scottish Rifles
1st East Surrey
1st DCLI
1st Norfolks

Position north to south:
123 Bty XXVIII Bde RFA
124 Bty XXVIII Bde RFA
122 Bty XXVIII Bde RFA
32 Bty XXVIII Bde RFA
37 Bty VIII (H) Bde RFA
80 Bty XV Bde RFA
11 Bty XV Bde RFA

Land above 600ft (200m)
Land above 500ft (150m)
Land above 300ft (100m)

0   1   2   3 Miles
0   1   2   3   4   5 Km

N

until midnight. He was unaware of what had happened at Landrecies, and assumed that I Corps would be close to Le Cateau covering his right flank in accordance with previous orders. The conviction grew upon him that he should consider fighting instead of retreating. A thorough infantryman, he felt that 'a stopping blow under cover of which we could retire,' was not merely possible, but essential.

Smith-Dorrien's belief that he should stand was reinforced when Allenby arrived to see him at 2am. Allenby's message was stark. His cavalry brigades were scattered, with men and horses 'pretty well played out'. Allenby believed that unless II Corps could move at once and get

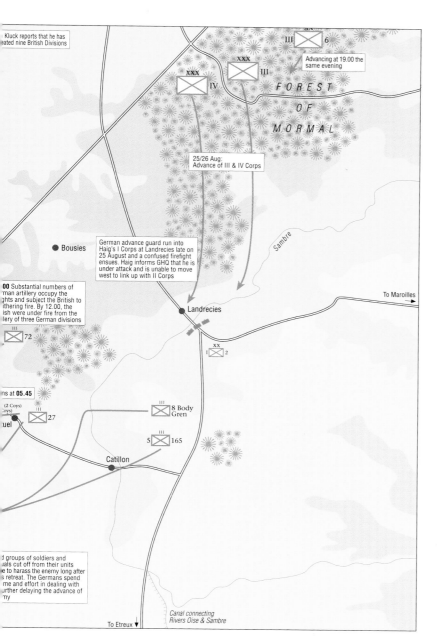

Kluck reports that he has eated nine British Divisions

III 6

Advancing at 19.00 the same evening

XXX III

XXX IV

FOREST

OF

MORMAL

25/26 Aug:
Advance of III & IV Corps

Sambre

● Bousies

German advance guard run into Haig's I Corps at Landrecies late on 25 August and a confused firefight ensues. Haig informs GHQ that he is under attack and is unable to move west to link up with II Corps

To Maroilles →

00 Substantial numbers of
man artillery occupy the
hts and subject the British to
ithering fire. By 12.00, the
ish were under fire from the
lery of three German divisions

III
72

● Landrecies

XX
I 2

ns at **05.45**

(2 Coys)
oys)
III
27
uel

III
8 Body
Gren

III
5 165

Catillon

d groups of soldiers and
uals cut off from their units
e to harass the enemy long after
s retreat. The Germans spend
me and effort in dealing with
urther delaying the advance of
ny

Canal connecting
Rivers Oise & Sambre

To Etreux ▼

away under cover of darkness, they would be forced to fight at dawn because the enemy were so near.

Smith-Dorrien sent for Gen. Hamilton, commander of the 3rd Division. Hamilton responded bluntly when asked if he could move his Division without delay. The earliest he could start would be 9am. Smith-Dorrien knew that what was true for the 3rd Division would apply also to the 5th and the 19th Infantry Brigades. He asked Allenby if he would be prepared to take orders and act as part of II Corps. Allenby assented at once. 'Very well, gentlemen,' Smith-Dorrien said calmly, 'we will fight and I will ask Gen. Snow to act under me as well.' Well aware of the fact that he was disobeying specific orders from GHQ, Smith-Dorrien's decision was a brave one. When he eventually learned that I Corps was still eight miles away and was continuing its retreat at first light, it was too late to change the orders again.

It was still a close thing. Smith-Dorrien personally went to 5th Division Headquarters to instruct Gen. Fergusson, while Allenby and Hamilton passed on the new orders to their own men. Both Fergusson and Snow were relieved at the decision to make a stand, but time was desperately short. Snow did not receive the changed instructions until 5am. Some units were already preparing to move out; others had no chance to make any form of defence other than hastily scraping shallow rifle pits in the rock-hard soil.

The battlefield

The battlefield of Le Cateau lacked the strings of mining villages and slag heaps as at Mons. It was open, undulating countryside which provided impressive fields of fire. Mons was an infantry battle. Le Cateau would be one in which artillery played the dominant role.

II Corps' position can be described as a flattened arrow head with a length of about ten miles, the point of which was at Caudry along the line of the Le Cateau to Cambrai road. To the left, 4th Division, composed of the 10th, 11th and 12th Brigades, faced north-west, forming what is technically known as a refused flank. Here they were in contact with the French Cavalry Corps under the command of Gen. Sordet who, in turn, maintained a link with Gen. d'Amade's Territorials who covered the gap all the way to the French coast. The French played an important, if rarely acknowledged, role that day by fighting off the German II Corps and preventing it from joining the main battle.

The centre of the line, from just east of Beauvois and running through Caudry and Inchy, was held by the 3rd Division facing slightly north-east. 5th Division continued the line which followed the road to Le Cateau and eventually curved round to face due east at the crossroads before the town itself. It was not a bad position, but the right flank was open. The 1st Duke of Cornwall's Light Infantry and two companies of the 1st East Surreys had been sent there to link up with Haig's I Corps.

Behind the infantry was the cavalry. The 4th Brigade was at Ligny behind the centre of the line. The 1st Brigade and some of the 2nd was on the right and the 3rd Brigade was away to the east trying to make contact with I Corps.

Against them, von Kluck sent four divisions drawn from III and IV Corps, the three divisions of II Cavalry Corps and, later in the day, the artillery and a further division of IV Reserve Corps. He still believed he was facing a BEF consisting of six divisions, all of which were in front of him. Obsessed with the idea that the BEF would try to make for the Channel ports (a not unshrewd reading of Sir John French's mind), he was convinced his enemy would be aligned in a north-south position between the Sambre and Cambrai. The encounters at Landrecies and Maroilles had done nothing to alter this belief.

Von Kluck's plan was simple. Both flanks would be attacked and the British crushed like a walnut between a pair of crackers. Von Kluck therefore ordered II Corps to Cambrai; von Marwitz's II Cavalry Corps, recalled from its wanderings in the west, was to hold down the left of the British position until the arrival of IV Reserve Corps. In the centre, IV Corps would divert attention from III Corps as it swung across to envelop the right of the British line. The result would be the simultaneous rolling up of both flanks and total destruction of the British force. As at Mons, however, von Kluck's troops ran piecemeal into the British positions and the battle was done before their full strength could be used.

The battle begins

Dawn came with a thick mist. It was 26 August, the anniversary of the battle of Crécy in 1346, when the English archers had each fired 12

Once news of the encounters with British troops reached Germany, there was a flood of illustrations depicting the battles. This spirited picture shows the German cavalry charging 'English Highlanders' - an imaginative concept - and is typical of many of this period. (Michael Solka)

arrows a minute to destroy their enemy; in 1914, the Short Lee-Enfield rifle would do the same task with 15 aimed rounds a minute.

The battle of Le Cateau began at about 6am as German artillery began a bombardment all along the British line. The lessons of Mons had been absorbed. The British infantry would be shelled into submission before the main assault began. The British artillery reacted swiftly, the guns coming right forward to protect their infantry. In the centre, the British troops strung out along the Le Cateau-Cambrai road endured stoically as the enemy artillery sought to pin them down while the main assaults hit the flanks.

On the right flank, the battle was especially fierce. It was here that the Duke of Cornwall's Light Infantry and East Surreys had tried to link up with I Corps. Having found no sign of Haig's men, they were formed up and ready to march off when they were surprised by German infantry. The Germans, from the 7th Division of IV Corps, had taken advantage of the dawn mist to infiltrate their way into and through Le Cateau itself. The ambush developed into a savage action as the British, fighting stubbornly in small groups, fell back along the Selle Valley towards the high ground south-east of the town. The 3rd Cavalry Brigade came up in support, as did 'L' Battery of the RHA. By noon, the detachment had rejoined the main body of its parent 14th Brigade. The action had cost 200 casualties, but the Germans made no attempt to pursue their quarry as they moved away from the valley. The German infantry pressed on along the Selle Valley. The mist hid their movements as they pushed out to occupy higher ground to the east, an area which would provide an excellent platform for the German artillery to enfilade their enemy.

It was not long before a very serious situation, fraught with danger for the British, developed. A successful German attack to the west of Le Cateau allowed them to move more artillery up to the high ground north of the Cambrai road. The British right flank was held by the 13th, 14th and 19th Brigades; the order to stand and fight had not reached brigade level when the German attack started and they were brought to combat in positions they had not anticipated holding.

The British artillery, on the ridges behind the infantry, came as close as it could to the front line, firing from just 1,200 yards into the German positions. They provided a prime target for their German counterparts who began to concentrate on destroying the British guns. The 11th Battery RFA, in particular, suffered heavily. By 10am the battery had lost all of its officers and only one gun was still in action. It was then that heavy German infantry assaults developed, huge masses pushing forward in overwhelming numbers.

By about 11am, the British positions along the ridge were enfiladed on both sides. The 2nd Suffolks and the 2nd King's Own Yorkshire Light Infantry, together with two companies of the 2nd Argyll and Sutherland Highlanders endured a hail of artillery and machine gun fire but, with an intense and desperate courage, they drove back every German assault.

The Royal Artillery gunners, firing 'as calmly as if they were on the practice

The BEF was poorly equipped with heavy artillery – another tribute to official parsimony – in comparison with its enemy and its ammunition was very largely shrapnel rather than high explosive. At full recoil this is one of the 16 60-pounders that accompanied the BEF to France. The total BEF establishment of artillery pieces of all calibres was 490 guns – less than the Germans concentrated for the siege of Namur alone! (Private Collection)

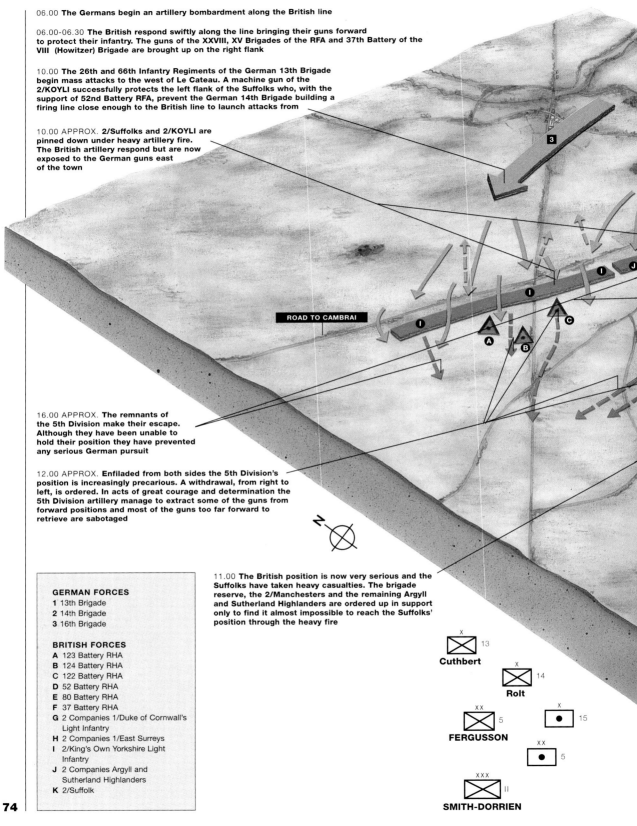

06.00 **The Germans begin an artillery bombardment along the British line**

06.00-06.30 **The British respond swiftly along the line bringing their guns forward to protect their infantry. The guns of the XXVIII, XV Brigades of the RFA and 37th Battery of the VIII (Howitzer) Brigade are brought up on the right flank**

10.00 **The 26th and 66th Infantry Regiments of the German 13th Brigade begin mass attacks to the west of Le Cateau. A machine gun of the 2/KOYLI successfully protects the left flank of the Suffolks who, with the support of 52nd Battery RFA, prevent the German 14th Brigade building a firing line close enough to the British line to launch attacks from**

10.00 APPROX. **2/Suffolks and 2/KOYLI are pinned down under heavy artillery fire. The British artillery respond but are now exposed to the German guns east of the town**

ROAD TO CAMBRAI

16.00 APPROX. **The remnants of the 5th Division make their escape. Although they have been unable to hold their position they have prevented any serious German pursuit**

12.00 APPROX. **Enfiladed from both sides the 5th Division's position is increasingly precarious. A withdrawal, from right to left, is ordered. In acts of great courage and determination the 5th Division artillery manage to extract some of the guns from forward positions and most of the guns too far forward to retrieve are sabotaged**

11.00 **The British position is now very serious and the Suffolks have taken heavy casualties. The brigade reserve, the 2/Manchesters and the remaining Argyll and Sutherland Highlanders are ordered up in support only to find it almost impossible to reach the Suffolks' position through the heavy fire**

GERMAN FORCES
1 13th Brigade
2 14th Brigade
3 16th Brigade

BRITISH FORCES
A 123 Battery RHA
B 124 Battery RHA
C 122 Battery RHA
D 52 Battery RHA
E 80 Battery RHA
F 37 Battery RHA
G 2 Companies 1/Duke of Cornwall's Light Infantry
H 2 Companies 1/East Surreys
I 2/King's Own Yorkshire Light Infantry
J 2 Companies Argyll and Sutherland Highlanders
K 2/Suffolk

x
13
Cuthbert

x
14
Rolt

xx
5
FERGUSSON

x
15

xx
5

xxx
II
SMITH-DORRIEN

74

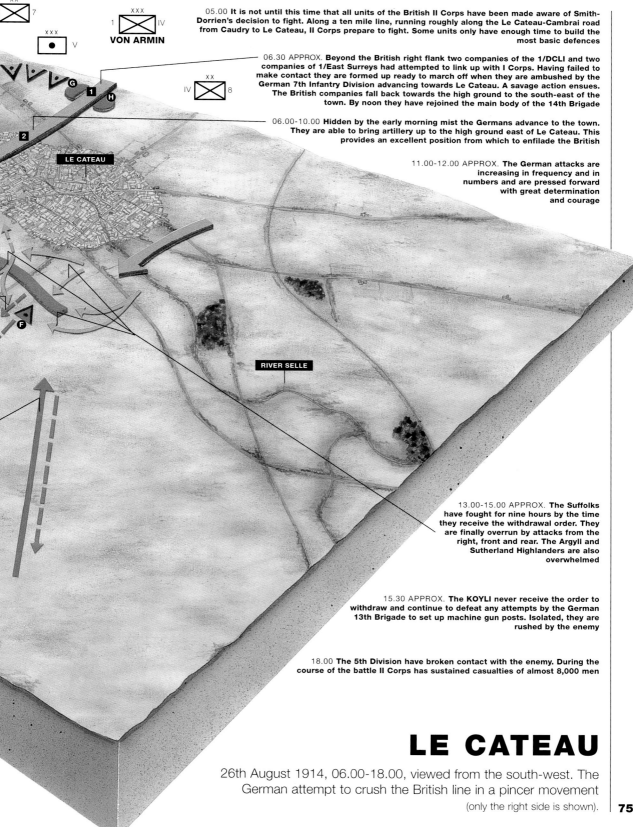

05.00 It is not until this time that all units of the British II Corps have been made aware of Smith-Dorrien's decision to fight. Along a ten mile line, running roughly along the Le Cateau-Cambrai road from Caudry to Le Cateau, II Corps prepare to fight. Some units only have enough time to build the most basic defences

06.30 APPROX. Beyond the British right flank two companies of the 1/DCLI and two companies of 1/East Surreys had attempted to link up with I Corps. Having failed to make contact they are formed up ready to march off when they are ambushed by the German 7th Infantry Division advancing towards Le Cateau. A savage action ensues. The British companies fall back towards the high ground to the south-east of the town. By noon they have rejoined the main body of the 14th Brigade

06.00-10.00 Hidden by the early morning mist the Germans advance to the town. They are able to bring artillery up to the high ground east of Le Cateau. This provides an excellent position from which to enfilade the British

11.00-12.00 APPROX. The German attacks are increasing in frequency and in numbers and are pressed forward with great determination and courage

VON ARMIN

LE CATEAU

RIVER SELLE

13.00-15.00 APPROX. The Suffolks have fought for nine hours by the time they receive the withdrawal order. They are finally overrun by attacks from the right, front and rear. The Argyll and Sutherland Highlanders are also overwhelmed

15.30 APPROX. The KOYLI never receive the order to withdraw and continue to defeat any attempts by the German 13th Brigade to set up machine gun posts. Isolated, they are rushed by the enemy

18.00 The 5th Division have broken contact with the enemy. During the course of the battle II Corps has sustained casualties of almost 8,000 men

LE CATEAU

26th August 1914, 06.00-18.00, viewed from the south-west. The German attempt to crush the British line in a pincer movement

(only the right side is shown).

Supplying the retreating BEF was a nightmare. The Quartermaster-General, Sir William Robertson, ordered his men to dump supplies at crossroads and along the routes down which the BEF would pass. This simple and inspired action saved many men who would otherwise have simply given up. Robertson holds the unique record of having held every rank in the British Army from cavalry trooper to field-marshal. (Author's Collection)

range', contributed to the maelstrom of defensive fire. Every attempt by the German infantry to develop a firing line and assault position close to the British was thwarted. The 122nd Battery was involved in an extraordinary incident when a platoon of German infantry came over a ridge in close formation. The battery fired a single salvo and the platoon was obliterated.

By a combination of fighting skill, quite exceptional courage and a fierce determination not to give way, the two infantry battalions forming the right flank of the British position held out against nine German infantry battalions, their supporting machine gun companies and the greater part of the artillery resources of three divisions.

An attempt to send the 2nd Manchesters and the remainder of the 2nd Argyll and Sutherland Highlanders forward as reinforcements virtually foundered as they came under intense German fire from the right flank. By noon, 11th Battery RFA had finally succumbed, its last gun being put out of action; the German infantry, still huge in numbers, was steadily and stealthily getting closer; the enemy's artillery fire was sweeping the British positions; and machine gun posts were raking the survivors. By every yardstick, the position was impossible to hold, but after six hours of intense fighting the line was still unbroken.

In the centre of II Corps' position, in the area of Caudry, there were no serious German attacks during the morning. Caudry had been the target of intense German shelling, but what little enemy infantry activity there was was quickly discouraged by the British defenders. The Germans succeeded briefly in occupying Inchy but were swiftly driven out. Throughout the morning, British casualties came to something under 200 men.

The left flank

On the left flank, it was a different tale altogether. It was here that the other half of the pincer envelopment was planned and where Gen. Snow's 4th Division, the new boys who had arrived in France just one week earlier and thus missed the advance to Mons, the battle there and its exhausting aftermath, had their first real taste of action. As on the right, the British were surprised. The 4th Division, without cavalry or cyclists, had little ability to mount far-ranging patrols. The area between them and Cambrai in the distance was patrolled by French cavalry; the first indication that anything was amiss was the sight of two distant French cavalrymen turning and galloping away. Almost immediately, heavy machine-gun and artillery fire hit the British positions.

The 1st King's Own were caught in the open, forming up in close formation to move to a new position, and their casualties were heavy. Lying down, their formation was such that only the front rank of each platoon could fire at their opponents, troops of the 2nd Cavalry Division. The King's Own lost 400 men within minutes, but were aided by the intervention of the 1st Hampshires to their right. Two companies of the 1st Royal Warwicks (among them a young subaltern by the name of Bernard Law Montgomery) forced their way forward in a brave but expensive gesture of support.

The 4th and 7th Jaeger Battalions quickly tried to outflank the British position. Supported by dismounted cavalry, the Jaegers swarmed forward, forcing the King's Own and the Hampshires to retire. Before the Hampshire pulled back, though, they demonstrated once more the telling power of British rifle fire. In open country, just 1,000 yards from their line, a German field battery set up position. In less than a minute, the concentrated fire of the Hampshires forced its retirement.

Even so, the Jaegers pushed hard. Moving on towards the battalions on the left of the position, the 2nd Lancashire Fusiliers and 2nd Royal Inniskilling Fusiliers, there was a fierce fire-fight which lasted some two hours. Supported by 21 machine guns, five batteries of horse artillery and the dismounted cavalry – who were not, according to some observers, over-enthusiastic about fighting on foot – they came very close indeed to rolling up the British position.

The 7th Jaegers enfiladed the Lancashires and moved on through a cornfield, unaware that the Inniskilling Fusiliers were waiting for them. Within seconds, the Jaegers were reeling back, with 47 dead lying amidst the ripened corn while the Inniskillings suffered not a single casualty.

The artillery of the German IV Reserve Corps was hurriedly brought up to contibute to the bombardment, which reached a new crescendo before a final, desperate assault. The familiar German mass, firing from the hip, surged forward with stubborn and determined gallantry only to be mown down by a torrent of fire. The Germans showed outstanding bravery, but were repulsed with heavy casualties. The defenders themselves suffered severe losses in an action which was savage in its intensity. By 10am, in the words of the British Official History, the two battalions 'had fought 2nd Cavalry Division to a standstill'.

In the same area, to the right, the 1st East Lancashires, 1st Rifle Brigade, 1st Somerset Light Infantry and 1st Hampshires, who comprised the 11th Brigade, all suffered badly under heavy artillery and small arms fire. They, too, held their ground in the face of repeated assaults, even venturing counterattacks. Sometimes driven from their line by savage shrapnel, they regained every position.

The retreat

There was now a mid-morning lull, punctuated by exchanges of fire between the opposing artillery and some unenthusiastic and ineffective attempts by the German infantry to go round the left flank of the 4th Division. Snow realised, however, that the time was fast approaching when he would have to disengage. His casualties were steadily mounting and the Germans would inevitably overwhelm his line.

On the right flank, affairs were becoming even more perilous. Although they had suffered heavy losses, the German infantry displayed a consistent gallantry and had, by late morning, enfiladed both flanks of the 5th Division. The German attack had been reinforced by their 5th Division of III Corps, and the British forces – four infantry battalions and two Royal Field Artillery brigades – faced the onslaught of at least 12 German infantry battalions and the combined artillery of three divisions. Under massive attack from the front and both sides, the situation shortly after noon was grim indeed. It was not surprising that some British soldiers began to slip away. Gen. Fergusson was acutely aware of the danger. There was no chance of reinforcement; the only choices were to die where they stood, or retire, and the retirement had to begin soon if it was not to become a rout.

Smith-Dorrien agreed and issued orders to all of II Corps to retire. The withdrawal would take place from right to left, 5th Division first, then the 3rd and finally the 4th. It was one thing to issue the order; it was another for it to reach the troops involved. With the very few available field telephone wires cut, orders had to be delivered personally. Messengers died as they tried to get forward through a torrent of shrapnel and bullets. It took 20 minutes for the retirement order to travel less than two miles, the distance between the headquarters of II Corps and 5th Division. It was another hour before it reached the front line units, and some never received it at all.

Saving the guns

The 5th Division units not involved on the ridge retired with little difficulty. The 15th Brigade and three battalions of the 14th Brigade pulled back without interference. It was a different story for the troops on the ridge. The first priority was to save the artillery. The guns were almost directly in the infantry's firing line, their crews having suffered so badly that none of the batteries were any longer capable of sustained action. It was now that some quite remarkable feats of gallantry

SAVING THE GUNS AT LE CATEAU, 26 AUGUST 1914
On the ridge to the south-west of Le Cateau the XV Brigade guns retreated under heavy fire. The 37th Battery had pulled back four out of six howitzers and no longer had sufficient horses and limbers to return for the

remaining guns. Once back at the rear, Captain Reynolds, the battery commander, called for volunteers to fetch the guns. Two teams set off, only one returned. For their gallantry Captain Reynolds and Drivers Luke and Drain received the Victoria Cross.

occurred. The 11th Battery teams galloped up during a lull in the fighting and retrieved five out of six of their guns. The sixth team was shot down by startled German infantry. The 80th Battery also retrieved five of its guns. The 52nd Battery had to abandon all of its guns as every team was brought down in the attempt.

Shortly afterwards, 122 Battery gathered their guns in a dashing action which 'brought the infantry cheering to their feet'. As the gun teams were sighted by the enemy, they were engulfed by shrapnel and bullets. The officer was killed and one team went down in a tangle of shrieking horses. Three guns were limbered up, two of them rattling away under a hail of fire. The third was shot to pieces, the horses being machine-gunned from German positions north of the Cambrai road. Four

guns were abandoned, surrounded by dead and wounded artillerymen and horses.

The guns of the 123rd and 124th batteries which were even further forward could not be saved. Their surviving crews removed the breech blocks and smashed the sights before abandoning them to the enemy.

The 37th Battery was able to claim, under persistent enemy fire, four out of six howitzers in its first foray. They could do no more as enemy action had already cut down the number of horses they had available. Once back at the rear, the battery commander, Capt. Reynolds, called for volunteers to rescue the two abandoned howitzers. Two teams returned. Both howitzers were limbered up under intense fire from German infantry, now only 100 yards distant. One team was brought down before it could move, but the other galloped clear with its howitzer. It was an act of astonishing gallantry and Capt. Reynolds, along with Drivers Luke and Drain, the survivors of the successful team, received the Victoria Cross. Driver Coby, the third member of the team, had been killed on the approach to the guns.

The withdrawal of the infantry was even more perilous. The Suffolks and the supporting Argylls and Manchesters faced enemy infantry, including the 26th Infantry at their front, their right and the rear. Overwhelmed, the survivors still managed to retire in relatively good order, fighting their way back and preventing every effort by the Germans to work their way round the flank.

The 2nd KOYLI, on the left of the Suffolks, never received the order to retire. They had already taken a severe hammering during the morning's action and their first intimation of the withdrawal was the sight of the German 66th Infantry approaching in mass down the ridge to their front. The British waited until the Germans were well within range before subjecting them to a withering fire which left the ground littered with dead and wounded. The retirement on their right meant that the KOYLI were swiftly surrounded. They continued a gritty defence, shooting down large numbers of German troops and stopping every enemy attempt to set up machine gun posts. The action of 'B' Company is typical of the battalion. Reduced to 19 men, faced with a surging mass of enemy troops advancing towards them, the company's commander, Maj. Yate, ordered his men to charge the enemy. They were, as one of their opponents acknowledged, 'incomparable soldiers'.

By about 4pm, it was all over for the survivors on the ridge. Their stubborn defence nonetheless paid enormous dividends, as they prevented any serious pursuit of the remainder of the 5th Division as it escaped down the Selle Valley and by six o'clock that evening, the 5th Division had successfully broken contact with the enemy.

In the centre, the 3rd Division came under severe attack during the afternoon. There had been heavy artillery fire throughout the morning. This intensified in the early afternoon and was combined with infantry attacks by elements of the 8th Division, 4th Cavalry Division and 9th Cavalry Division. The outskirts of Caudry were occupied by the enemy, but an attack to the east, on Audencourt, was thwarted at a heavy cost to the German infantry.

Every day of the Retreat from Mons brought more casualties. This one stands beside a Quarter-master sergeant of the Royal Army Medical Corps. (Private Collection)

The 3rd Division began its retirement at about 3.30pm with little interference from the Germans, although the area was still being shelled. The artillery suffered some losses: the 107th and 108th Batteries each lost a section, and a German salvo destroyed three complete teams of the 6th Battery as it withdrew. As on the right flank, however, there were communication problems. The 1st Gordons, in the very centre of the British line at Audencourt, together with two companies of the 2nd Royal Irish and some 2nd Royal Scots, were the rearguard of the 8th Infantry Brigade. The order never reached them so they simply stayed put and fought off every attack that was launched against them.

German troops from the 8th Infantry Division advanced across a field of beetroot, only to run into devastating fire from the Scots. For an hour, the Germans tried to break through but failed; they attempted to outflank the British position but, as darkness approached, their casualties were so high that the whole attack stalled. This bought enough time for the rest of the 3rd Division to move away. By midnight the commanding officer, Col. W.G. Gordon VC, decided it was time to leave. Moving through the darkness, the Gordons ran into substantial enemy forces and after a heavy exchange of fire were forced to surrender.

For the 4th Division, retirement was a little more difficult. The Germans had withdrawn the 2nd and 9th Cavalry Divisions and replaced them with the 7th Reserve Division of the IVth Reserve Corps which had made a forced march from Valenciennes. These fresh troops came forward vigorously, pushing the 11th Brigade back to Ligny. The rearguard, 1st Rifle Brigade, supported by XIV and XXIX Brigades of the RFA, stopped the German advance with such purpose that the attack on Ligny petered out. Caught in the open, the Germans suffered very severely from the combined onslaught of the British infantry and artillery.

The German commander then tried to turn the British flank, but was foiled by the arrival of the artillery attached to the French Cavalry Corps under Gen. Sordet. Their vicious 75mm guns threw the German attackers into disarray and the 4th Division started to disengage. There was great confusion as the infantry pulled out, units becoming intermingled or finding themselves surrounded by advancing German troops. Two companies of the 1st Royal Warwicks had an interesting time. For the next three days, they marched between the German cavalry screen and its following infantry, moving only by night and hiding by day, until they were able to rejoin the BEF.

II Corps was severely mauled at Le Cateau. The official casualty figures show Smith-Dorrien lost 7,812 men and 38 guns. German losses are not known. No figures are available, and estimates range from 15,000 to 30,000 dead, wounded and missing. Without doubt, the casualties were very severe. Von Kluck was convinced that he had been fighting all six divisions of the BEF, as well as its cavalry and several French Territorial divisions. The next morning his pursuit was to the south-west as he was still positive the British would make for the Channel ports.

II Corps went southwards with the luxury of a 12 hour start. For the rest of the retreat, as Smith-Dorrien himself wrote, II Corps 'were no more seriously troubled … except by mounted troops and mobile detachments who kept at a respectful distance'. No soldier in II Corps afterwards ever believed anything other than that they had saved the BEF from utter defeat. Smith-Dorrien's gamble had paid off.

AFTERMATH

t was not the end. The retreat continued and it was a hard road. I and II Corps drifted apart for a while on the long plod south, being separated by about 15 miles before their paths once again converged. There were days when bitter meetings left huddled bodies in khaki or field-grey in the fields and woods of France.

Etreux

There was a fiercely contested action at Etreux on 27 August when the Guard Cavalry Division of I Cavalry Corps and X Reserve Corps came upon the rearguard of 1 Division. The 2nd Royal Munster Fusiliers, aided by two guns of 118 Battery RFA and two troops from 'C' Squadron of the 15th Hussars, fought for nearly 12 hours against a minimum of nine German battalions and four artillery batteries. The Munsters vanished from the British Order of Battle, the only survivors being the remnants of two platoons.

Néry

At Néry, the 1st Cavalry Brigade, made up of the Queen's Bays, 5th Dragoon Guards and 11th Hussars, with the ubiquitous 'L' Battery of the RHA, was surprised in the early morning mist on 1 September by the 4th Cavalry Division. Heavy artillery and small arms fire from a ridge outside the village hammered into the Bays – whose horses stampeded – and the RHA gunners. Three of 'L' Battery's guns were soon disabled; the sur-

This photograph is of British troops lining a roadside ditch. This bears a strong resemblance to the northern French countryside, but the distance between the riflemen is a not inaccurate portrayal of the meagreness of the British line. (Private Collection)

viving crewmen helped man the three remaining. One was quickly knocked out. The other two kept firing until every member of its crew was dead or wounded. The last gun continued to fight on for nearly an hour despite the combined fire of 12 German guns against it.

At last, manned by Capt. Bradbury, the 2 i/c of 'L' Battery, Battery Sgt.-Maj. Dorrell and Sgt. Nelson, the lone gun came to the end of its resistance. Bradbury was mortally wounded fetching ammunition; Nelson and Dorrell fired their last shell at 8.10pm. All three were awarded the Victoria Cross. Meanwhile, the rest of the Brigade reacted sharply. 'L' Battery had covered them as they worked their way round the

The graves of Captain Bradbury VC and Lieutenant John Campbell at Néry, photographed a few days after the action. The Nèry action was publicised throughout the world, one account appearing in a Mexican newspaper. The story so aroused the admiration of a Japanese businessman resident in Mexico that he commissioned three signet rings, each engraved with the word 'Hero' in Japanese script, for presentation to the families of three selected participants. One of these was Lieutenant Campbell. German accounts of the battle insisted that the 4th Cavalry Division was greatly outnumbered by British infantry columns supported by cavalry and artillery. (Imperial War Museum)

German flanks where they pinned down the enemy. Fresh troops arrived. The 4th Cavalry Brigade, 'I' Battery of the RHA, the 1st Middlesex and part of 10th Infantry Brigade came up and opened an annihilating fire on the ridge, forcing the Germans back in great disorder. Eight of the German guns were abandoned where they were, and the other four were found next day in a nearby wood. The German 4th Cavalry Division was so badly damaged that it was withdrawn from the Cavalry Corps and sent to the IV Reserve Corps.

'L' Battery lost three officers killed and two wounded, 20 men killed and 29 wounded, a total of 54 out of the 135 British casualties at Néry.

Villers-Cotterêts

That same day, the rearguard of the 2nd Division, at Villers-Cotterêts about 15 miles east of Néry, came into brutal contact with advance troops of III Corps and the 2nd and 9th Cavalry Divisions. The rearguard, the 4th (Guards) Brigade, was on the northern edge of a forest, criss-crossed by wide tracks which provided natural fields of fire. From about 10.45am onwards, there was a hard and confused battle among the woodland as the Guards struggled clear. The early attacks hit the 2nd Coldstream and the 1st Irish Guards. Col. Morris, the CO of the Irish Guards, was killed by a machine gun burst. Two platoons of the 2nd Grenadier Guards were surrounded and fought to the end. The brigade lost more than 300 officers and men, and the 6th Brigade, which covered the Guards withdrawal, lost another 160.

The BEF went on to halt the German offensive later in the month at the battle of the Marne, forcing them to retreat to the Aisne. Later in the autumn, the BEF turned north again and found themselves at Ypres. It was to be the graveyard of the old British Regular Army.

'L' Battery, RHA, just before embarkation for France in 1914. In the action at Néry, three of its members were to win the Victoria Cross. Twenty three would be killed and 31 wounded, thus effectively removing the unit from the BEF Order of Battle. (Imperial War Museum)

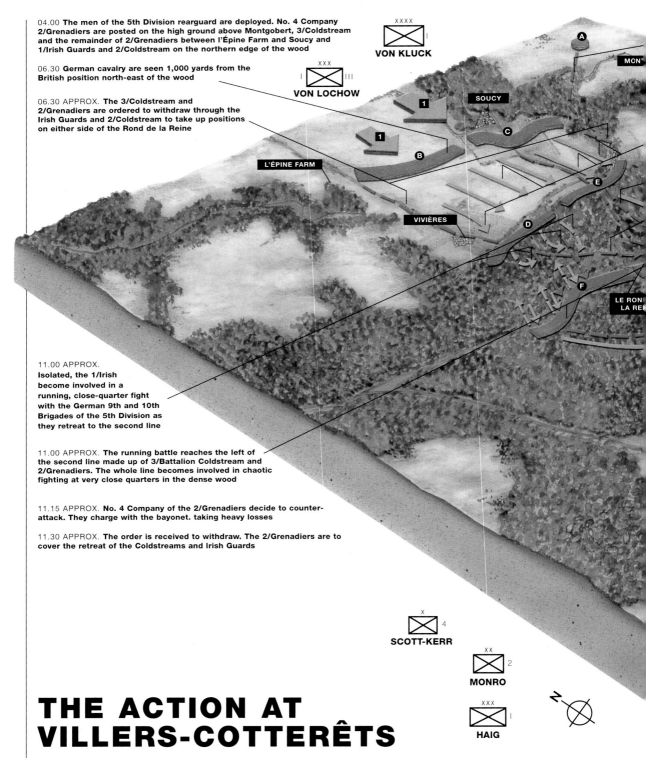

04.00 The men of the 5th Division rearguard are deployed. No. 4 Company 2/Grenadiers are posted on the high ground above Montgobert, 3/Coldstream and the remainder of 2/Grenadiers between l'Épine Farm and Soucy and 1/Irish Guards and 2/Coldstream on the northern edge of the wood

06.30 German cavalry are seen 1,000 yards from the British position north-east of the wood

06.30 APPROX. The 3/Coldstream and 2/Grenadiers are ordered to withdraw through the Irish Guards and 2/Coldstream to take up positions on either side of the Rond de la Reine

11.00 APPROX.
Isolated, the 1/Irish become involved in a running, close-quarter fight with the German 9th and 10th Brigades of the 5th Division as they retreat to the second line

11.00 APPROX. The running battle reaches the left of the second line made up of 3/Battalion Coldstream and 2/Grenadiers. The whole line becomes involved in chaotic fighting at very close quarters in the dense wood

11.15 APPROX. No. 4 Company of the 2/Grenadiers decide to counter-attack. They charge with the bayonet. taking heavy losses

11.30 APPROX. The order is received to withdraw. The 2/Grenadiers are to cover the retreat of the Coldstreams and Irish Guards

VON KLUCK

VON LOCHOW

SOUCY

L'ÉPINE FARM

VIVIÈRES

MON

LE RON
LA RE

SCOTT-KERR

MONRO

HAIG

THE ACTION AT VILLERS-COTTERÊTS

1 September 1914, 06.30-14.00 approx., viewed from the south-west showing the attack by the German 3 Corps on the rearguard of the British 2nd Division retiring through the thick wood at Villers-Cotterêts. The wood is crisscrossed with rides many of which come to a junction at the Rond de la Reine; the rides provide the only, limited, field of fire.

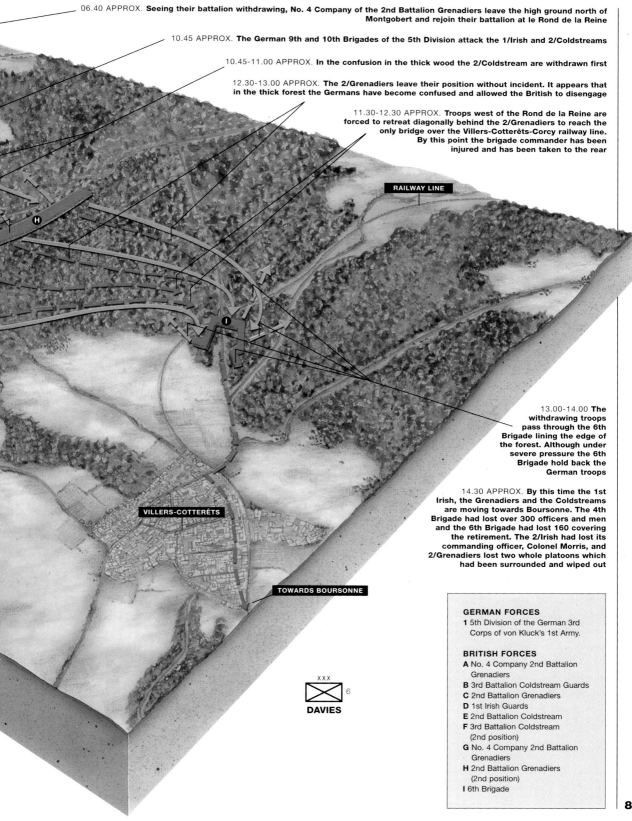

06.40 APPROX. **Seeing their battalion withdrawing, No. 4 Company of the 2nd Battalion Grenadiers leave the high ground north of Montgobert and rejoin their battalion at le Rond de la Reine**

10.45 APPROX. **The German 9th and 10th Brigades of the 5th Division attack the 1/Irish and 2/Coldstreams**

10.45-11.00 APPROX. **In the confusion in the thick wood the 2/Coldstream are withdrawn first**

12.30-13.00 APPROX. **The 2/Grenadiers leave their position without incident. It appears that in the thick forest the Germans have become confused and allowed the British to disengage**

11.30-12.30 APPROX. **Troops west of the Rond de la Reine are forced to retreat diagonally behind the 2/Grenadiers to reach the only bridge over the Villers-Cotterêts-Corcy railway line. By this point the brigade commander has been injured and has been taken to the rear**

RAILWAY LINE

13.00-14.00 **The withdrawing troops pass through the 6th Brigade lining the edge of the forest. Although under severe pressure the 6th Brigade hold back the German troops**

14.30 APPROX. **By this time the 1st Irish, the Grenadiers and the Coldstreams are moving towards Boursonne. The 4th Brigade had lost over 300 officers and men and the 6th Brigade had lost 160 covering the retirement. The 2/Irish had lost its commanding officer, Colonel Morris, and 2/Grenadiers lost two whole platoons which had been surrounded and wiped out**

VILLERS-COTTERÊTS

TOWARDS BOURSONNE

XXX
6
DAVIES

GERMAN FORCES
1 5th Division of the German 3rd Corps of von Kluck's 1st Army.

BRITISH FORCES
A No. 4 Company 2nd Battalion Grenadiers
B 3rd Battalion Coldstream Guards
C 2nd Battalion Grenadiers
D 1st Irish Guards
E 2nd Battalion Coldstream
F 3rd Battalion Coldstream (2nd position)
G No. 4 Company 2nd Battalion Grenadiers
H 2nd Battalion Grenadiers (2nd position)
I 6th Brigade

87

WARGAMING MONS

The heady days of August 1914 have always been popular with both boardgamers and miniatures players. The opening weeks of the Great War are effectively the end of the 'horse and musket' era. Rifle-armed infantry still manoeuvre by battalions, supported by horse-drawn artillery, and, for the last time, cavalrymen hear the spine-tingling order 'Draw Swords!'.

At a tactical level, this period is at once visually appealing and intellectually challenging. Reasonably complete ranges of figures are available in 25-, 15- and 5mm scales, and important troop types over-looked by the manufacturers are easily converted from nineteenth century ranges. (For instance, my 15mm Belgian infantry began life as Austrian infantry for 1866.) At operational level, the challenge of manoeuvring the BEF in the path of the oncoming juggernaut soon generates great sympathy for Sir John French and, indeed, the commanders of the other armies. The German commanders are under terrible pressure, trying to sustain a very optimistic march schedule in the face of some very stubborn opponents and an intractable logistics problem. The French try to make a fighting withdrawal with an army trained and armed for the offensive, while the Belgians make a gallant defence in the face of overwhelming numbers. Misunderstandings and personality clashes occurred within each army as well as between notional allies, offering great scope for multi-player games.

Tactical games

The Mons campaign witnessed a succession of small-scale actions of the sort that easily fit on a wargames table. The epic defence of Néry, the Guards brigade's rearguard action at Villers-Cotterêts and the 5th Cavalry Brigade at Cérizy all involve a handful of battalions/squadrons against larger (although equally exhausted) German forces. Obviously, if you re-fight these specific actions the Germans must be constrained from taking advantage of hindsight; historically, they never knew exactly what they were facing. In north-east France during high summer, the frequent early morning mists hampered aerial reconnaissance and enabled rear-guards to withdraw or ambush their pursuers at will.

As a foot- or saddle-sore German advance guard pressed onwards, it would frequently deliver a hasty attack wherever opposition showed itself. However, a few British infantry companies or cavalry squadrons could deliver a formidable weight of fire. Determined resistance or even a spirited counter-attack (like the charge of the 12th Lancers at Cérizy) often led the Germans to conclude they were facing much larger forces, in the same way von Kluck believed he had fought the whole BEF at Le Cateau.

A representative scenario might feature a British infantry or cavalry brigade deployed on a map, with figures placed on the table only when

The roads leading south towards Paris were clogged with troops and refugees. Some idea of the difficulties involved in moving along them can be gleaned from this picture. The road is narrow. A cavalry troop is coming one way, a line of army carts and civilians is going the other. Many roads were unsurfaced. Dry, they gave off a swirling mass of dust but became a morass as soon as there was heavy rain.

their location is revealed by firing or by Germans blundering into close combat. They would seldom occupy anything more than shell-scrapes, as men who had been marching all day and half the night had neither the time nor inclination to dig more comprehensive defences. Incidentally, Walter Bloem's account of Mons confirms that this was not a 'British disease': the 12th Brandenburg Grenadiers were equally reluctant to entrench even when a British counter-attack threatened. German forces, say a cavalry brigade followed by an infantry division, arrive on table in dribs and drabs. I write unit identities on index cards, add some blanks and draw one per (hourly) turn. Some cards provide a cavalry regiment, others a whole infantry brigade. The British, of course, are ignorant as to what they are facing until it hoves into view. What might have begun as a successful rearguard operation might turn to catastrophe if powerful German reinforcements arrive in time to outflank and trap the defenders. As the Munsters discovered, withdrawal from close contact with such an enemy is all but impossible. However, this sort of débâcle can be the beginning of an alternative scenario where a cut-off detachment attempts to break through the German forces to safety.

When framing a set of miniatures rules, or modifying a commercially-available one, the *Field Service Pocket Book 1914* is an invaluable aid, providing vital data on lengths of marching columns, the times required to prepare field defences etc. One item deserves emphasis: in both board- and figure-games, defenders of buildings are generally harder to hit than troops in the open. Reality is not quite so simple, especially not in 1914. At Mons and Le Cateau, British infantry usually dug their shell scrapes in front of the built-up areas, not actually in the villages themselves. As contemporary manuals stressed, early 20th-century artillery could hit buildings from far beyond the range of rifles, with catastrophic consequences for the defenders, unless the buildings had been thoroughly prepared for defence. Unless the defenders had 24 hours to clear out combustible material and entrench themselves in the basement, occupying a building simply offered the enemy an easily identified target. By contrast, shallow trenches in the open were harder to spot and more difficult for the gunners to range on. Fire from such positions a few hundred yards in front of a village was usually mistaken for fire from the buildings, leading the enemy to shell the village and leave the infantry relatively unscathed.

The armies of the Mons campaign had different tactical doctrines, which should be recognised in any tactical level wargame. German battalions usually led with one company in open order, one in support and

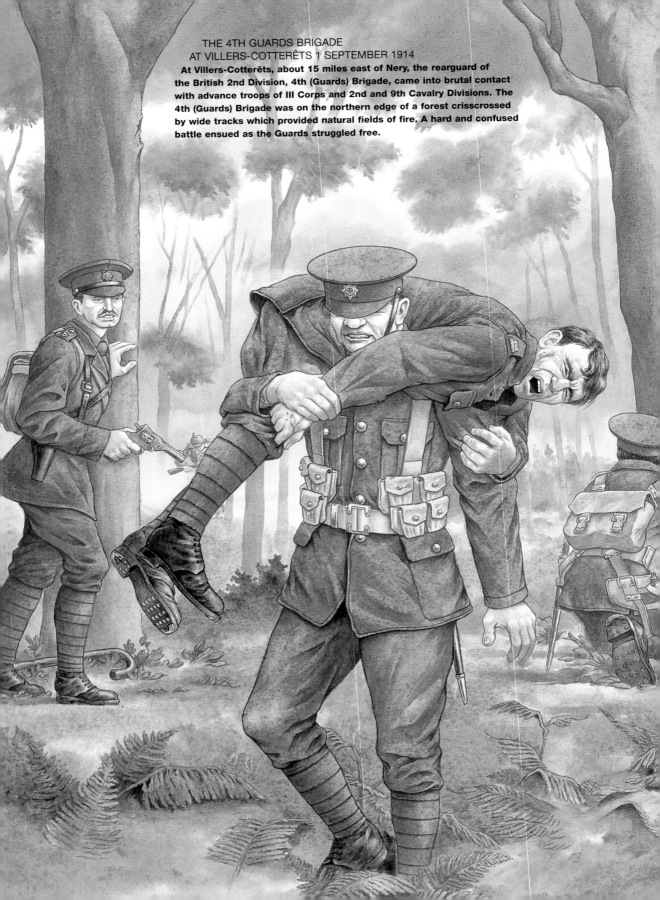

THE 4TH GUARDS BRIGADE
AT VILLERS-COTTERÊTS 1 SEPTEMBER 1914

At Villers-Cotterêts, about 15 miles east of Nery, the rearguard of the British 2nd Division, 4th (Guards) Brigade, came into brutal contact with advance troops of III Corps and 2nd and 9th Cavalry Divisions. The 4th (Guards) Brigade was on the northern edge of a forest crisscrossed by wide tracks which provided natural fields of fire. A hard and confused battle ensued as the Guards struggled free.

the other two following in shoulder-to-shoulder lines several hundred yards behind. Some soon learned that deployment in greater depth was required to avoid the beaten zone of the defenders' rifles. The British followed a similar approach. Even on the defensive, the British were supposed to be in three lines: a firing line with about one yard per man was bolstered by supports in the rear who reinforced the line as casualties mounted. The third wave was not supposed to reinforce the line, but was intended for counter-attacks as a defence by fire alone was unlikely to prove decisive.

German casualty figures during the first weeks of the war are impossible to determine accurately. These wounded are amongst the early casualties. (Author's Collection)

The French notoriously neglected open order tactics and their rifle fire was notably less accurate. Their cavalry had little enthusiasm for dismounted action and short-range carbines gave them little incentive to try. (The lack of bayonets also made them helpless in close combat on foot.) However, their fabled 75mm guns lived up to pre-war expectations. British observers noted that the French tended to give up ground easily, but as often as not recapture it by counter-attack, whereas the British would doggedly hold the same position: which method was less costly was impossible to determine.

Some British accounts of the Mons campaign suggest the Germans had learnt nothing from the war of 1870 and describe waves of German infantry attacking in close order as if magazine-loading rifles had never been invented and the Boer War had never happened. Yet on other parts of the same battlefield, German infantry might come on in thin skirmish lines, developing an effective attack with excellent support from their artillery. This was a consequence of the extraordinary degree of autonomy allowed to pre-war German corps commanders. They reported directly to the Kaiser, the famed General Staff having operational control in war, but not the power to dictate training standards or tactical doctrine. Like most other armies, the pre-war German Army had been sharply divided over the tactical lessons of both the Boer War and the Russo-Japanese War. Scattering infantrymen over wide frontages might reduce losses in the short term, but (some argued) it made command and control impossible, led to the whole unit becoming paralysed in the face of the enemy and eventually to greater casualties in the long term. The opposing view, based on studies of the Russo-Japanese war accepted that close formations would suffer heavier losses, but, still under control of their officers, they could continue to manoeuvre and deliver fire. Only a close formation had the group spirit required to close with the bayonet – and it was the threat of cold steel,

The fighting in France and Flanders brought home the reality of war to a British public which previously had considered battles to be affairs which took place in far-off lands against primitive natives. Even the Boer War had not changed that attitude a great deal. This altered when the wounded from Mons, Le Cateau and the Retreat were brought back to England and crowds gathered to stare as the casualties were ferried from the railway stations to hospital. It was a sight that was to become commonplace in the four years that followed. (Private Collection)

not long-range rifle fire that would finally eject a defender from his position. Since the pre-war training of the troops would not be under the control of the player, you can dice for their formation when German troops arrive on the battlefield or even when they deliver an attack. Close formations should be more likely to keep moving, but they are better targets and under effective fire they will break up.

German accounts of the Mons campaign testify to the effectiveness of British rifle fire, but both sides soon recognised that this was going to be an artillery war. Gunners recognised three types of firing position in 1914: open, semi-covered and covered. The former is self-explanatory. In a semi-covered position, the gun would be far enough behind a crestline for the gun itself (but not the muzzle-flash) to be concealed from the enemy. In a fully covered position both the gun and the flash were hidden. Covered positions were much easier for howitzer batteries than the flat trajectory field guns which could only fire from such defiladed positions at the cost of a long stretch of dead ground in front of the gun. Unless this space was covered by infantry, the enemy could work his way under the line of fire with terrible consequences for the artillery.

Horse-teams were horrifically vulnerable targets. We have seen how the incredibly brave attempt to save the guns of 37th (Howitzer) battery at Le Cateau resulted in no fewer than three VCs, which suggests some idea of the hazards involved. More than one infantry officer watching team after team gallop forward to its death said it reminded them of Balaklava.

Mounted reconnaissance was difficult enough in the face of machine guns and magazine-loading rifles, but it was the improved long range accuracy of quick-fire artillery that really frustrated the cavalry. Time and again, German cavalry regiments operating dismounted against a British rearguard saw their lead horses dispersed by British artillery fire. The German cavalry were reluctant to continue advancing when this happened, but in the gently rolling ground of the French/Belgian border, it was not always possible to find cover for the horses.

Mons-Le Cateau in an afternoon

By sacrificing the finer details of the tactical battle, Mons or Le Cateau can be re-fought in an afternoon's game session. As usual, some thought must be given to stopping the Germans exploiting the fact that, unlike the historical German commanders, they know what they are facing.

Mons and Le Cateau were hardly the first instances of a numerically superior force failing to crush a smaller army because they overestimated the enemy's strength. Antietam springs to mind. Boardgamers can find some readily tailored solutions in previous game designs like Peter Perla's area movement game of Antietam. Here, the overwhelmingly superior Union army uncoils so slowly that a nimble Confederate defence can fend them off until nightfall – usually. But if the turns last longer, the Federals sometimes manage to concentrate their striking power and Lee is driven off the map and into the Potomac.

For Mons or Le Cateau the use of hidden movement is essential. (Is that line of counters pushing past the flank just another bunch of blanks or is it the Prussian Guard?) Have game turns of uncertain duration: on average it is not possible for the Germans to move anything like their full strength, but the possibility is there for a succession of long turns which could spell doom for the 'contemptible little army'.

Multi-player games

The utter confusion of August 1914 is perhaps best simulated by a multi-player game. Not just the chaos prevailing at headquarters where exhausted officers puzzled over reports that were necessarily out of date by the time they arrived, but the added friction between very different nations (the British and the French) and abrasive personalities (Sir John French, Kitchener, Smith-Dorrien etc.).

Unlike modern staffs, there was no duplication in a 1914 headquarters. It was not possible to have part of an HQ on the move while the remainder ran the battle. Generals and their staffs found themselves riding to and fro all day, then writing orders all night. Having only an hour or two to sleep in every 24 soon told on the toughest constitutions. Lack of sleep can turn the most congenial of men irritable. It certainly helped poison relations between the suspiciously anglophobic Lanzerac and Sir John French, and it did nothing for the latter when Grierson was replaced not by the friend he had requested (Plumer), but his old enemy, Smith-Dorrien. Sir Horace himself was notorious for his vile temper and his rages were a legend in the Edwardian army (and the likely reason he did not become C.-in-C. India despite his brilliance as a soldier). This potent brew of personalities cries out for a matrix game system or other species of role-play. The objective here is not to recreate that fatuous burlesque, *O What a Lovely War!*, but to bring out the very real problems of coalition warfare. The BEF could be forgiven for thinking that French policy was to defend the Third Republic down to the last Englishman. Lanzerac was not the only Frenchman to dwell on the fact that his nation was providing 90 per cent of Allied manpower on the Western Front.

Whichever way you choose to wargame this fascinating period, remember the words of the British staff study of Le Cateau: 'Perhaps the most important lesson of all is that, no matter how unfavourable conditions may appear, nor how desperate the situation may seem, the enemy is probably in a worse plight and the combatant with the real will to win will always achieve victory.'

THE BATTLEFIELD TODAY

The single day encounters of Mons and Le Cateau left no mark on the landscape. Behind the German lines during 1914-1918, they survived relatively unscathed, although new housing, a motorway and other contemporary building have sliced across and along the lines of the scenes of the Old Contemptibles' actions. It is still possible, even today, to see the area much as the original members of the BEF saw it.

Mons itself is a bustling town, but the Grande Place, with its imposing town hall, is not greatly changed; even allowing for modern traffic, there are areas which are much the same as they were in 1914. The Musée du Centenaire, in the Jardin du Mayer, houses the World War One and Two collections and is just off the Grande Place. There are plans to rehouse the collection in due course.

The Paris motorway now runs alongside the canal but the towpath is accessible and buildings still remain which served as aid posts or battalion headquarters on that desperate August day. It needs little imagination to envisage how things were for you can stand where the British gunners sweated and swore, and look across at the tree line from where German soldiers dressed in field-grey advanced towards the dry-mouthed British infantry.

Much of the Le Cateau battlefield remains as it was when the BEF fought there. The ditches along the Roman road which became cover for the rifles of the infantry as they halted the German attacks remain much as they were. Beetroot still grows in the silent fields at Audencourt over which the German soldiers advanced so bravely in the summer sun in 1914.

The area can be toured by car, but the enthusiast might prefer to use a bicycle which makes a number of the remoter locations more easily accessible. It is especially useful for covering the full length of the canal at Mons. Both the Mons battlefield, which extends along a 25-mile line, and the shorter Le Cateau line repay study. The local tourist offices can give information about hiring bicycles locally.

Rose Coombs' invaluable guide to the battlefields, *Before Endeavours Fade*, gives detailed itineraries and should be an essential part of any visitor's baggage. Accommodation across a wide price range can be found; again, the local tourist offices give an excellent service, but it should be remembered that many places are now important commercial centres and the town hotels are geared to business customers, not battlefield visitors, and their prices reflect this. There are, though, many smaller places to stay in the villages, as well as several camping areas.

A number of sites are on farm land or private property. It is an accepted courtesy to seek permission before tramping over them and it cannot be too highly recommended that even a few words of execrable French, Dutch or Flemish, are invaluable in obtaining the goodwill of the landowner.

FURTHER READING

Many books have been written by participants and later historians about the events of August 1914. Unfortunately, a great many of them are now out of print, although copies can often be obtained from specialist dealers. Many of the British accounts, especially those written during the inter-war years, not only dismiss all French and Belgian participation in the war, but grossly overstate the importance of Mons and Le Cateau. One writer goes so far as to call Mons 'the battle that saved the world', a panegyric that one suspects the old BEF would have found embarrassing. The following are a tiny selection of useful titles in English and which are obtainable without too much difficulty via specialist dealers or the library service.

Ascoli, David, *The Mons Star* (Harrap, 1981)
> A worthwhile and well-researched account, often drawing on personal reminiscences of the BEF in 1914. Interestingly, Ascoli is condemnatory of the French Commanders, a prejudice which reflects the feeling of the BEF at the time.

Bloem, Walter, *The Advance from Mons* (Peter Davies, 1930)
> Most of the German accounts of the early days of the war are palpably inaccurate and the official records are sometimes positively misleading. This memoir, written by an officer of the Brandenburg Grenadiers and widely quoted by many English writers because of the tributes it pays to the BEF, is nonetheless one of the few that gives a realistic idea of what it was like to come under the 'mad minute' rifle fire of the British professional soldier.

Coombs, Rose, *Before Endeavours Fade* (Plaistow Press, 1994)
> This latest edition of Rose Coombs' guide to the First World War battlefields should always be to hand. Originally published in 1976, the guide has been extensively revised.

Edmonds, Brigadier J.E., *Official History, France & Belgium, 1914 – Volume 1.* (Macmillan, 1926)
> An invaluable, indeed indispensable, tool for the student. Edmonds' work in compiling the Official History can rarely be faulted, although in his non-official capacity, he had a great talent for creating mischief.

French, Field Marshal Viscount, *1914*
> French's own account of the events of 1914 reveals his distrust, bitterness and paranoia and, like the memoirs of Lloyd George, is a source more to its author's character than anything else.

Simpson, Keith, *The Old Contemptibles* (George Allen & Unwin, 1981)
> A photographic history of the BEF from August to December 1914. This is a slim volume with a necessarily truncated text and its real interest lies in the illustrations.

Spears, Sir Edward, *Liaison 1914* (Heinemann, 1930)
> Spears had an uncanny habit (too uncanny, according to some observers) of being in the right place at the right time, and so witnessed some of the momentous happenings on the BEF front which he describes vividly and with brilliant detail. His book is an invaluable source work, although his personal prejudices sometimes shade his narrative.

Terraine, John, *Mons, 1914* (Batsford, 1960)
> One of the best accounts. Well researched and eminently readable.

Tuchman, Barbara, *The Guns Of August* (Constable, 1962)
> A comprehensive work dealing with the events leading up to the outbreak of war and the battles of 1914, both in the East and West. The author is not unnaturally fascinated by the personality clashes and politics of the period, sometimes at the expense of military events, and occasionally puts too much reliance on some dubious sources.